How to Train Your
Beagle

liz palika

BEAGLE

Photos by the author unless
otherwise credited.

The Publisher would like to thank the owners of all the dogs in this book,
including Arne Aamodt, Valerie Barabas, Daniel Bell, Lee Cord, Lorraine
Delahanty, L. Forrest, Teresa Gaier, Terri Gainetti, Bruce and Shirley Irwin,
Elizabeth Meszaros, Ruth Stewart, Anita Tillman, and Charles Timpone.

© T.F.H. Publications, Inc.

Distributed in the UNITED STATES to the Pet Trade by T.F.H. Publications,
Inc., 1 TFH Plaza, Neptune City, NJ 07753; on the Internet at www.tfh.com;
in CANADA by Rolf C. Hagen Inc., 3225 Sartelon St., Montreal, Quebec H4R
1E8; Pet Trade by H & L Pet Supplies Inc., 27 Kingston Crescent, Kitchener,
Ontario N2B 2T6; in ENGLAND by T.F.H. Publications, PO Box 74, Havant
PO9 5TT; in AUSTRALIA AND THE SOUTH PACIFIC by T.F.H. (Australia), Pty.
Ltd., Box 149, Brookvale 2100 N.S.W., Australia; in NEW ZEALAND by
Brooklands Aquarium Ltd., 5 McGiven Drive, New Plymouth, RD1 New
Zealand; in SOUTH AFRICA by Rolf C. Hagen S.A. (PTY.) LTD., P.O. Box
201199, Durban North 4016, South Africa; in JAPAN by T.F.H. Publications,
Japan—Jiro Tsuda, 10-12-3 Ohjidai, Sakura, Chiba 285, Japan. Published by
T.F.H. Publications, Inc.

MANUFACTURED IN THE
UNITED STATES OF AMERICA
BY T.F.H. PUBLICATIONS, INC.

contents

INTRODUCTION

As a dog obedience class instructor, I see a variety of breeds in my classes. Lots of breeds gain or lose popularity over the years, but some breeds remain relatively stable in number. Beagles are one of those breeds. I usually have at least one and sometimes two or three Beagles in any basic obedience class.

Usually the Beagles do well in training, but once in a while I see a situation where the dog and owner are both unhappy, and I can tell the situation is going to get worse. Usually, this is the result of the owner not understanding what a Beagle is before he acquires one.

A Beagle is a short-haired, small breed of dog. Many people don't look any further than that and get a Beagle for those attributes alone. What

Most people are interested in Beagles because of their small size, energetic nature, and short hair. They don't often realize that Beagles are also excellent hunting dogs.

beagle

Photo by Isabelle Francais

Beagles are known for their boundless energy. Before purchasing a Beagle, make sure that you are aware of all the breed's characteristics and special needs.

beagle

Most people don't realize that Beagles are natural hunting dogs. They also have very loud voices.

they don't realize is that a Beagle is a hunting dog—a small one, granted—but still a hunting dog. In addition, this is a pack hound that was designed to hunt in a pack of Beagles, and he has a very loud voice that can cause great havoc with nearby neighbors!

It's important that potential Beagle owners understand the Beagle's nature before buying one. This is a very nice breed of dog, but he is certainly not for everyone. Beagle owners also need to know how to train their dog so that he can fit into their lives as smoothly and quietly as possible.

In this book, I have tried to present Beagle owners (and prospective Beagle owners) with realistic options about choosing a Beagle and good information about training that dog. A Beagle can be a wonderful family pet and companion, as well as a super hunting dog. With help from their owners, Beagles can be friends, partners, and great companions.

SELECTING
the Right Dog for You

WHAT ARE BEAGLES?

Dogs have been used to hunt for hundreds of years, and scent hounds have hunted for food to feed their owners for as long as dogs have been domesticated. However, Beagles as we know them today probably originated as smaller versions of the English Foxhound. Large foxhounds were used to hunt not just foxes, but other game, too, including deer. Not everyone was allowed to hunt deer—that was restricted to royalty—so smaller dogs were used to hunt rabbits and hares. Rabbits and hares were not only food for the table but destructive pests that threatened the farmers' livelihood. Braces (two dogs) or packs (several dogs) of Beagles could help control the damage that the pests could cause.

In early America, versatility was important in all dogs. The

In early America, braces (two dogs) or packs of Beagles were used to hunt rabbits and hares, which were not only used as food, but were destructive pests that threatened farmers' livelihood.

Photo by Isabelle Francais

early settlers couldn't have a dog with just one skill or ability, because they needed a dog that could do many things. The Black and Tan Hound was a popular hunting dog of early settlers, and this dog was used to hunt just about anything that needed hunting, including rabbits. This dog was often crossbred with other similar dogs—as often happened in early America—and Beagles were often used as the other breeding partner. This produced a smaller, more versatile hunting dog.

In the mid-1800s, American Beagle fanciers were importing packs of quality Beagles from England. These dogs were used as foundation breeding stock. General Richard Rowett of Illinois was an avid Beagler and bred for a beautiful, hard-working, hard-hunting scent hound.

The National Beagle Club of America was formed in 1887, and the first Beagle field trial was held in 1888 in Hyannis, Massachusetts. Field trials, hunting events, and specialty shows have been held on a regular basis since then.

THE BEAGLE TODAY

Beagles today come in two varieties: dogs under 13 inches tall at the shoulder and dogs

---

FAMOUS BEAGLE OWNERS
Charles Schultz, the creator of the cartoon "Peanuts" is probably one of the most famous Beagle owners. Snoopy, of that comic strip, is obviously a Beagle! Other famous Beagle owners include the football player and announcer, Roger Staubach, actresses Mary Pickford and Eva Gabor, and singer Barry Manilow.

---

between 13 and 15 inches tall. Other than height, the two varieties are basically the same.

The Beagles today are still hounds and look much like Foxhounds in miniature. They should give the appearance of being able to follow a trail through brambles and brush with good stamina and lots of strength. A Beagle is square, with the length of back equal to the dog's height. He has a deep chest, with room for the big lungs and heart necessary for a good athlete. When at a trot, the Beagle should move gracefully, with a fluid motion; again, giving the appearance of an athlete.

The Beagle's head should be slightly domed but broad. The ears are set low and are long and heavy, reaching almost to the tip of the nose if pulled forward. The eyes are large, set well apart, and dark. The soft,

Photo by Isabelle Francais

Beagles should appear to be athletic and graceful and possess a small but sturdy build. Coat colors range from lemon and white to chocolate.

beagle

Photo by Robert Pearcy

Beagles make great family pets because of their patience and their ability to interact well with children.

hound-like, pleading eyes are very expressive.

Beagles come in a variety of colors, although the white with tan markings and black saddle across the back is most common. Beagles can also be lemon and white, red and white, chocolate, tan and white, and even ticked. "Ticking" is when the black saddle or blanket has flecks of color. For example, if a white, tan, and black-saddled Beagle has gray and white flecks of color in the black saddle, that Beagle is then called a "blue-ticked" Beagle.

THE BLUE-TICKED BEAGLE

A blue-ticked Beagle gets his name only because of his coloring; it is not a mix of a Beagle and Blue-Ticked Coonhound—a common misconception.

TEMPERAMENT

The appearance of the Beagle attracts many people. Their small size, short coat, and appealing hound look suits many people. In addition, Beagles are usually very good with children and are very patient, traits that parents like. Unfortunately, some of the breed's other traits can make them somewhat less desirable as pets.

Benjamin L. Hart, DVM, and Lynette A. Hart, authors of *The Perfect Puppy*, said, "Beagles rank in the lowest percentiles for ease of obedience training and ease of housetraining." In other words, compared to many other popular breeds, Beagles do not always accept training well. This does not mean that Beagles are untrainable—far from it. But it does mean that the owners of a Beagle must figure out how to motivate a Beagle to want to be good so that life is not a constant argument!

The Harts continued by saying, "The Beagle ranks high in the tendency to exert dominance over the owner." As a pack dog, pack order is very important to Beagles, and if a Beagle with a more dominant personality senses a weakness in the human pack leaders, he will assert his own dominance. This means the owners of Beagles must be aware of this tendency and work to avoid it.

The Beagle is not a watchdog and was not bred for that purpose, so potential owners should not get a Beagle for that reason. Beagles do bark, and sometimes bark quite loudly and for long periods of time, but they do not usually limit their barking to trespassers and intruders.

A Beagle alone in the backyard is a lonely dog, isolated and away from his pack. A Beagle alone will bark and howl. However, two Beagles could do quite well together.

A Beagle is usually not a cuddly dog, so if you are looking for a dog to snuggle at your feet and follow you from room to room, a Beagle is not the best choice. Beagles do need to spend time with people, especially as puppies, so that they bond well with their owners, but a Beagle will never be a snuggler like many other breeds.

IS A BEAGLE THE RIGHT BREED FOR YOU?

Evaluating Your Personality and Lifestyle

Adding a dog to your family

Because Beagles prefer to stay within packs, owning more than one Beagle might be beneficial. A lonely Beagle that feels isolated from his pack could become a problem barker.

Photo by Isabelle Francais

Beagles enjoy being outside in the fresh air. Taking your Beagle (or Beagles) out for a run in the grass is a great way to spend quality time together.

is like adopting a new family member. This is a 14-year obligation that should not be taken lightly. Take some time to think about this commitment prior to adding a dog to your family.

Do you work long hours, come home tired, and would rather relax than do anything else? You should probably adopt a pair of older Beagles. Two could keep each other company when you aren't home, and older dogs would be less energetic and less demanding of you.

Do you come home tired but enjoy doing things outside? Two younger adult Beagles might suit you. Again, two could keep each other company while you're at work, but younger dogs would be willing to go places and do things with you when you're at home.

Do you have a flexible schedule, work short hours, or spend a lot of time at home? In this situation, a puppy might be the right choice for you.

Some people get a dog so that they can be the center of someone's world; they love the companionship of a dog and the

Although Beagles like affection, they are not the type of dog that will constantly want to be by your side.

All dogs have specific needs. Before you purchase a Beagle, make sure that you are aware of the breed's special requirements.

devotion that many dogs show their owners. If you want a dog who will follow you from room to room, always lying at your feet and wanting to be close to you at all times, then don't get a Beagle. A Beagle will know where you are, in what room and how far away, but doesn't necessarily need to follow you there. Now if you go to the kitchen, the Beagle will be right there underfoot, but there's some additional motivation to be there!

The Beagle's Needs

All dogs have some specific requirements, and before you get a Beagle, think about these needs. It could make the difference between a successful relationship and the need to give the dog up later.

First of all, remember that Beagles are pack dogs. They were designed to hunt with another Beagle or a pack of Beagles. A Beagle is not a good dog to have alone. If you love the breed and really want a Beagle but cannot spend most of the day with your dog, then you should consider having two.

You must be willing to spend time exercising your Beagle. These are active dogs bred to hunt rabbits. They need daily vigorous exercise.

Your Beagle also needs a good training program. He needs to learn social and household rules, and you need to be able to

Photo by Vince Serbin

If you can't supervise your Beagle, it's a good idea to build him a dog run or put up a fence. He needs to exercise on a daily basis and this will allow him to do so even if you are not home.

control his barking and howling so that you don't have any complaints from your neighbors.

Your Beagle also needs a securely fenced yard or dog run. As a hunting dog, Beagles follow their nose and do not always think about where their nose is leading them. That could be out of the yard, down the block, across the busy street, or far, far away. Beagles need a secure fence to protect them from themselves.

SELECTING THE RIGHT DOG

Male or Female?

There are a lot of myths concerning the traits of males and females. Ultimately, it

depends on the personality of the individual dog. Spayed bitches (females) and neutered dogs (males) are usually a little calmer than those that are not; spaying and neutering removes the sexual hormones and as a result, the sexual tension that can accompany those hormones. To be a good pet and companion, your dog doesn't need those hormones anyway.

A DOG RUN
A fenced-in area that is 6 feet wide by 20 feet long is fine for two Beagles. Bigger is better, of course, but this size is adequate. The run should be secure, covered (if possible), and offer protection from the sun and inclement weather.

Male Beagles do tend to be a little bigger than females and slightly heavier boned. Because the Beagle is not a big dog anyway, this doesn't make much difference.

Male Beagles can mark their territory by lifting their leg and urinating, which can be an annoying habit. Neutered males do tend to do it less, and training can help control it.

What Age?

Puppies are adorable, including Beagle puppies. However, puppies are a lot of work. Puppies eat, sleep, relieve themselves, play, relieve themselves again, and then start the whole cycle all over.

When you add a puppy to the family, you need to count on at least two years of puppyhood before the Beagle is mature (mentally as well as physically). When your Beagle is fully grown, you will have a wonderful friend and companion, but it will require two years of your time and effort to get to that point.

If you aren't sure you have the time, patience, and energy to raise a puppy, think about getting an adult dog instead. Many adult Beagles need new homes—perhaps an owner passed away or was transferred overseas—and these dogs can make very good pets.

Just as with raising a puppy, there are some negative factors

It's true that puppies are adorable, but they do require a lot of work. Be aware of a puppy's needs before you decide to purchase one.

to think about before adopting an adult dog. Adopting an adult dog can be compared to buying a used car: sometimes you get a gem, sometimes you get a lemon. You don't know how the dog was treated prior to adoption. Many times the dog's past treatment, training (or lack thereof), and even health care can affect his future behavior.

You must also be willing to be patient with the dog while he settles into your household. It takes newly adopted dogs at least three months to settle down. Until the dog realizes he's there for good, you won't see his real personality and behavior.

Finding an Adult Dog

If you have decided that an adult dog would be a better choice for you than a puppy, there are a few places where you can look for that dog. Check at your local humane society or animal shelter. Most people who give up their dog leave the dog at a shelter. You can also check the classified advertisements in your local newspaper or the bulletin boards at the veterinarian's office.

Evaluating an Adult Dog

Once you have found an adult Beagle, how do you decide whether this dog is right for you? First of all, do you like the dog?

RESCUE GROUPS

Most breed clubs sponsor or run breed rescue groups. These groups screen the dogs they take in for adoption as to personality, temperament, and training. This prescreening can be beneficial, because it will give you a head start when deciding if this dog might be the right one for you. Dogs handled by rescue groups are also vaccinated, spayed or neutered, and examined for other health problems. Your local shelter can give you the phone number of a Beagle rescue group.

Your feelings for the dog are certainly going to play a big part in any future relationship. If you don't like the dog now, don't expect that to change later.

Do you know why this dog was given up by his owner? A dog can be given up for many reasons that are no fault of his own. However, if the dog was given up because of behavior problems, you need to know that. Perhaps the dog barked too much and the neighbors complained. Maybe the dog wasn't housetrained or hasn't had any obedience training. These are important issues.

What is the dog's personality like? When you whistle, does the dog cock his head to the side and look at you? Does he come up to visit with you? If he comes up to

The way a dog behaves when you first meet him is a major indication of his personality. Having personalities that complement each other is a vital part of a healthy dog/owner relationship.

you wagging his tail, that is great. However, if he looks sideways at you, slinks, or bares his throat, be careful. This Beagle is worried, fearful, or shy and could potentially be a problem. If the dog stands on his tiptoes and stares at you, leave him alone. He's challenging you and could be potentially aggressive.

Ideally, you want a dog that is happy to see you without showing worry, fearfulness, or any aggression. You want a dog that is housetrained and hopefully has had some obedience training. Make sure the dog's behavior problems are ones that you can live with for the time being, until you have time to teach the dog.

Finding a Puppy

If you have the time and patience to raise a puppy, wonderful! You will want to find a reputable breeder from whom to buy a puppy so that you can get the best puppy possible. Breeder referrals can come from many places. Perhaps a neighbor has a nice Beagle; ask her where she got her dog. Your veterinarian might have a client whose Beagle produces nice healthy puppies. You may also want to attend a dog show in your area to talk to Beagle exhibitors there.

Once you find a few breeders, make an appointment to talk with them. At this meeting, ask a few questions: "Are you active in shows or dog sports?" Someone who shows her dogs in conformation dog shows will have dogs that are good representatives of the breed. If she competes in obedience trials, her dogs are trainable. However, if she runs her Beagles in a hunting pack, they may not be the best choice for you if you're looking for a suburban pet.

"Do you belong to the national or regional Beagle clubs?" Most clubs publish newsletters or magazines that contain articles concerning the breed's health and well-being.

"What health problems have you seen in your breed?" Beagles are healthy dogs, but a line with no problems whatsoever is unusual. The breeder should be honest with you about potential health threats and what she's doing to prevent them.

"Can you provide me with a list of references?" Of course she will give you references to people that are happy with her dogs, but that's okay, too. You can still ask them questions. Did the breeder follow through with everything she agreed to supply, including the puppy's paperwork? Would you buy another puppy from her?

Caring breeders will ask you as many questions as you asked her. She will want to make sure you are the right person for her puppy. Don't get defensive; instead, answer them truthfully. If by some chance she says her dogs are not right

LAB RESCUES

Because of their small size and hearty dispositions (among other attributes), Beagles are still used as laboratory dogs. These dogs are subject to a variety of tests, most of which we really don't want to think about. Once in a while an animal research group will rescue some of these dogs and offer them up for adoption. As much as it seems like a worthwhile and rewarding thing to do, be sure to think twice before adopting one of these dogs. These dogs have not had any socialization outside of the laboratory and are often afraid of everyday sights and sounds. They are usually not housetrained, have not had obedience training, and may or may not have been handled well during their lab life. If you can handle their shortcomings, go ahead and adopt one. However, make sure you do so with your eyes wide open and know what you're getting into.

Photo by Isabelle Francais

A good breeder will be honest with you about his or her dogs' health conditions. You want your Beagle to be as healthy as possible.

for you, listen to her. She knows her dogs better than you do, and she's probably right!

Evaluating a Puppy

Each puppy has his or her own personality, and finding the right personality to match with yours can sometimes be a challenge. If you are outgoing, extroverted, and active, a quiet, withdrawn, shy puppy would not fit well into your household. That puppy would do better in the household of a person who is just as quiet as he is.

When you go to look at a litter of puppies, you can do a few simple "tests" that can help you evaluate each puppy's temperament. Take one puppy away from his mom and littermates. Place him down on the ground and walk a few steps away. Squat down and call him to you. An outgoing, extroverted puppy will come to you and try to climb into your lap. If you stand up and walk away, the extrovert will follow you, trying to get underfoot. If you throw a piece of crumpled paper a few feet away, he will go after the paper, shake it, and try to shred it. This puppy will do well with someone who is just as much an extrovert as he is. He will need lots of exercise, good training, and a job to occupy his mind.

The quiet, submissive puppy will come to you when you call but may do a belly crawl or roll over to bare his belly. When you walk away, he may follow you, or he may watch you but hesitate to follow you. When you throw the paper, he may go after it, but hesitate to bring it back. This puppy will need a quiet owner, positive training, and gentle handling.

These two puppies are extremes for Beagle

beagle

Photo by Isabelle Francais

Observing a puppy away from his littermates can help you evaluate his temperament. An extroverted puppy will come right to you, while a more submissive puppy may do a belly crawl or roll over for a tummy rub.

Adding a Beagle to your family is a lifelong commitment. Make sure that you can provide your new Beagle with everything he needs in order to grow into a healthy and well-adjusted adult.

BE CAREFUL

Beagles live to an average of 14 years of age. Adding a Beagle to your family is a 14-year commitment to this dog's care, so make sure it's the right decision. Think it through very carefully, and only when you know it's the right decision should you bring home a dog.

Photo by Isabelle Francais

temperaments, and most are somewhere in between these two extremes. Try to find a puppy with a personality like your own. Do not get a quiet puppy and hope that you can liven him up. Nor should you get the extroverted puppy and think that you can calm him down. It won't work. Instead, get the puppy that is right for you.

Canine
DEVELOPMENT
Stages

IN THE BEGINNING

Hunting dogs, including hounds such as Beagles, have a long history of working and living with mankind. In spite of this shared history, the bond that we have with dogs must be renewed with each puppy. The bond itself is not hereditary, although the tendency to bond is. This relationship is what makes owning a dog so special, but it doesn't happen automatically. To understand when and how this bond develops, it's important to understand that your Beagle is a dog, not a person in a fuzzy dog suit.

Families and Packs

Most researchers agree that the ancestors of today's dogs were wolves, but they disagree on what wolves those ancestors were. They were either the ancestors to today's gray wolves or perhaps a species of wolf that is now extinct. In any event, wolves are social creatures that live in an extended family pack. The

As this floppy-eared trio demonstrates, Beagles are perfectly happy hanging out with each other.

Photo by Isabelle Francais

pack might consist of a dominant thing while our body language says something else. To our dogs, we are very complex, confusing creatures. We can say that both dogs and humans live in social groups, and we can use that comparison to understand a little more about our dogs; however, we must also understand that our families are very different from a wolf pack.

Because Beagles are bred to be a pack dog, the pack is very important to them. You've heard of the term a "one-person dog?" That rarely, if ever, applies to a Beagle. To your Beagle, one-person is rarely as important as the family or family pack.

FROM BIRTH TO FOUR WEEKS OF AGE

For the first three weeks of life, the family and the pack are unimportant as far as the baby Beagle is concerned. The only one of any significance is his mother. She is the key to his survival and the source of food, warmth, and security.

At four weeks of age, the baby Beagle's needs are still

Although a young puppy depends on his mother for all of his basic needs, his littermates provide him with warmth and security and help him build relationships with other dogs.

Photo by Isabelle Francais

Between the ages of five and seven weeks, a puppy goes through many changes. He starts to recognize people and individual voices. He is also playing more with his littermates.

being met by his mother, but his littermates are becoming more important. His brothers and sisters provide warmth and security when their mother leaves the nest. His curiosity is developing, and he will climb on and over his littermates, learning their scent and feel. During this period, he will learn to use his sense of hearing to follow sounds and his sense of vision to follow moving objects.

His mom will also start disciplining the puppies—very gently, of course—and this early discipline is vitally important to the puppies' future acceptance of discipline and training.

The breeder should be petting and playing with the puppies now to get them used to gentle handling. The puppies at this age can learn the difference between their mother's touch and a person's touch.

WEEKS FIVE THROUGH SEVEN

The young Beagle goes through some tremendous changes between five and seven weeks of age. He is learning to recognize people and is starting to respond to individual voices. He is playing more with his littermates, and the wrestling and scuffling teach each puppy how to get

At the age of eight weeks, most pups experience their first period of fear. It's wise to keep the puppy with his littermates for one more week before bringing him to a new home.

along, how to play, when the play is too rough, when to be submissive, and what to take seriously. His mother's discipline at this stage of development teaches the puppy to accept corrections, training, and affection.

The puppies should never be taken from their mother at this stage of development. Puppies taken away now and sent to new homes may have lasting behavior problems. They often have difficulty dealing with other dogs, may have trouble accepting rules and discipline, and may become excessively shy, aggressive, or fearful.

LET THE MOTHER DOG CORRECT

Some inexperienced breeders will stop the mother dog from correcting her puppies, perhaps thinking that the mother dog is impatient, tired, or a poor mother. When the mother dog is not allowed to correct the puppies naturally, the puppies do not learn how to accept discipline and have a hard time later when their new owner tries to establish some rules. Orphaned puppies raised by people suffer from the same problems. The mother dog knows instinctively what to do for her babies, and sometimes a correction—a low growl, a bark, or a snap of the teeth—is exactly what is needed.

THE EIGHTH WEEK

The eighth week of life is a frightening time for most puppies. Puppies go through several fear periods during the maturation process, and this is the first one. Even though this is the traditional time for most puppies to go to their new homes, they would actually benefit by staying with their littermates for one more week. If the puppy leaves the breeder during this fear period and is frightened by the car ride home, he may retain that fear of car rides for the rest of his life. In fact, this stress is why so many puppies get carsick!

It's important to provide your dog with a nutritionally fortified diet geared toward his stage of life. Look for foods that are naturally preserved, contain no by-products, and are 100 percent guaranteed. Photo courtesy of Midwestern Pet Foods, Inc.

The same applies to the puppy's new home, his first trip to the veterinarian's office, or anything else that frightens him.

WEEKS NINE THROUGH TWELVE

The baby Beagle can go to his new home anytime during the ninth and tenth weeks of life. At this age, he is ready to form permanent relationships. Take advantage of this and spend time with your new puppy, playing with him, and encouraging him to explore his new world. Teach him his name by calling him in a happy, high-pitched tone of voice. Encourage him to follow you

by backing away from him, patting your leg, and using your voice.

Socialization is very important now. Socialization is more than simply introducing your puppy to other people, dogs, noises, and sounds. It is making sure your baby Beagle is not frightened by these things as you introduce them. For example, once your baby Beagle has had some vaccinations (check with your veterinarian), take him with you to the pet store when you go to buy dog food. While there, introduce your puppy to the store clerks, other customers, and even to the

Disciplining your Beagle puppy at an early age will result in a well-behaved and properly socialized adult dog.

store parrot. Your trip there could also include walking up some stairs, walking on slippery floors, and going through an automatic door. All of these things, introduced gradually, with encouragement, and repeated all over town (on different days, of course!), add up to a confident, well-socialized puppy.

During this stage of development, your Beagle puppy's pack instincts are developing. He is beginning to understand who belongs to his pack or family and who doesn't. Do not let him growl at visitors during this stage. He

is much too young to understand when and how to protect. Instead, stop the growling and let him know that you—as his pack leader—can protect the family.

You can show him his position in the family in several different ways, but one of the easiest is to lay him down, roll him over, and give him a tummy rub. This exercise may seem very simple, but by baring his tummy, he is assuming a submissive position to you. When his mother corrected him by growling or barking at him, he would roll over and bare his tummy to her, in essence telling her, "Okay! I understand, you're the boss!" When you have him roll over for a tummy rub, you are helping him understand the same message, but you are doing it in a very gentle, loving way.

During this stage of development, discipline is very important. Love, affection, and security are still important, too, of course, but right now your Beagle puppy needs to learn that his life is governed by rules. Don't allow him to do anything now that you won't want him to continue doing later as a full-grown dog.

WEEKS THIRTEEN THROUGH SIXTEEN

From 13 through 16 weeks of age, your Beagle puppy will be trying to establish his position in your family pack. If you were able to set some rules in earlier stages of development, this won't be quite so difficult. However, if you cave in to that adorable Beagle face, well, this could be a challenging time!

Consistency in enforcing household rules is very important now, and everyone in the family or household should be enforcing the rules the same way. Beagles are very perceptive, and if your puppy senses a weak link in the chain of command, he will take advantage of it. This doesn't mean he's a bad puppy—it simply means he's smart.

Puppies with dominant personalities may start mounting behavior on small children in the family or on the puppy's toys. Obviously, this is undesirable behavior and should be stopped immediately. Just don't let it happen.

Socialization with other people, with friendly dogs, and other experiences should continue throughout this stage of development.

RETRIEVING

Begin retrieving games at 9 to 12 weeks of age. Get your Beagle's attention with a toy he likes and then toss it four to six feet away. When he grabs the toy, call him back to you in a happy tone of voice. Praise him enthusiastically when he brings it back to you. If he runs away and tries to get you to chase him, stand up and walk away, stopping the game completely. Don't chase him! Let him learn now, while he's young, that he must play games by your rules. Chasing a ball or soft flying disc can be great exercise for the puppy, and teaching him to play by your rules sets the stage for a sound working relationship later.

WEEKS SEVENTEEN THROUGH TWENTY SIX

Sometime between 17 and 26 weeks of age, most puppies go through another fear period, much like the one they went through at 8 weeks of age. Things the puppy had accepted as normal may suddenly become frightening. A friend's Beagle walked into the backyard and began barking fearfully at the picnic table that had been there in the same spot since before the puppy joined the family. It was as if the puppy had never noticed it before and all at once it was very scary!

Photo by Isabelle Francais

Beagles are not considered overly protective or aggressive dogs. However, they will bark to protect their pack or family.

beagle

Make sure you don't reinforce any of these fears. If you pet or cuddle him and tell him softly, "It's okay, sweetie, don't be afraid," he will assume these are positive reinforcements for his fears. In other words, your puppy will think he was right to be afraid. Instead, walk up to whatever is scaring him and let him see you touch it. Then tell him, "Look at this!" in a happy, fun, playful tone of voice so that he can see the thing he is afraid of really isn't scary at all.

Your Beagle's protective instincts will continue to develop through this stage. If your Beagle continues to show protectiveness or aggression (by growling, snarling, barking, or raising his hackles), interrupt his behavior by turning him away or distracting him. If you encourage this behavior this early or if you correct it too harshly, you will put too much emphasis on it and your puppy may continue to do it. Too much emphasis this young may result in overprotectiveness or fearfulness in your dog as he grows up. Instead, react with calmness and just stop it from happening.

Beagles are not naturally overly protective as adults. They do bark to defend their pack or family but are not naturally aggressive, protective dogs. At this age, however, your Beagle puppy doesn't know what or when to protect. Instead of letting him take over and learn bad habits, stop his behavior and let him know you are in charge.

THE TEENAGE MONTHS

The teenage months in a dog's life are very much like the teenage years in a human child's life. Human adolescents are feeling strong and are striving to prove their ability to take care of themselves. They want to be independent, yet they still want the security of home. These two conflicting needs seem to drive some teens (and their parents) absolutely crazy.

Dogs can be very much the same way. Beagles in adolescence push the boundaries of their rules, trying to see if you really will enforce those rules. Most Beagle owners say their dogs in this stage of growing up act "too full of themselves!"

The teenage stage in Beagles usually hits at about 12 months of age, although it's not unusual to see it happen a month or two earlier. You'll

Photo by Isabelle Francais

rough with children or chasing the cat.

During this stage of development, you really need to consistently enforce social and household rules. Hopefully, you will have already started obedience training because that control will help. If you haven't started obedience training, do so now—don't wait any longer.

Make sure, too, that your dog regards you as the leader. This is not the time to try and be best friends—that would cause a dominant personality to regard you as weak. Instead, act like the leader. Stand tall when you relate to your dog. Bend over him (not down to him) when you pet him. You should always go first through doorways or up the stairs and make him wait and follow you. You should always eat before you feed him.

Although your Beagle is your best companion, establish your role as the leader. If you act like his equal, he will take a dominant role in the relationship and be more difficult to train.

know when it happens. One day you will ask your previously well-trained dog to do something he knows very well, such as sit, and he'll look at you as if you're nuts. He's never heard that word before in his life and even if he had, he still wouldn't do it!

Other common behavior includes regression in social skills. Your previously well-socialized Beagle may start barking at other dogs or jumping on people. He may start getting

As the leader, you can give him permission to do things. For example, if he goes to pick up a toy for you to throw for him, give him permission to do it, "Good boy to bring me your toy!" If he lies down at your feet (by his own choice) tell him, "Good boy to lie down!" By giving him permission and praising him, you are putting yourself in control, even though he was already doing it of his own accord.

You need to understand that this rebellion is not aimed toward you, personally. Your Beagle is not doing this to you. Instead, it is a very natural part of growing up. Keep in mind that this, too, shall pass. Your Beagle will grow up, some day. Adolescence usually only lasts a few months (in dogs, anyway).

GROWING UP

Beagles are not usually considered fully mature—mentally and physically—until they are two years old. And even then, some Beagles still behave like puppies for even longer. Usually, the females act mature a little earlier than the males.

After the teenage stage but before maturity, your Beagle may go through another fear period. This usually hits at about 14 months of age but may occur later. Handle this one just like you did the others—don't reinforce your dog's fears. Happily, this is usually the last fear stage your dog will have.

There may be another period at about two years of age when your dog challenges you to see if you really are the boss. Treat this as you did the teenage stage; enforce the rules and praise what he does right.

When your Beagle reaches his second birthday, throw a party! He is usually considered grown up now.

By the age of two years, Beagles are considered fully mature—mentally and physically. Females tend to mature more quickly than males.

Photo by Isabelle Francais

beagle

Early
PUPPY
Training

HOUSETRAINING

Crate Training

By about five weeks of age, most puppies are starting to toddle away from their mom and littermates to relieve themselves. You can use this instinct to keep his bed clean, and with the help of a crate, you can housetrain your Beagle puppy. A crate is a plastic or wire travel cage that you can use as your Beagle's bed. Many new Beagle owners shudder at the thought of putting their puppy in a cage. "I could never do that!" they say, "It would be like putting my children in jail!" A puppy is not a child, however, and he has different needs and instincts. Puppies like to curl up in small dark places. That's why they like to sleep under the coffee table or under a chair.

Because your Beagle puppy has the instinct to keep his bed clean, being confined in the crate will help develop more bowel and bladder control. When he is confined for gradually extended periods of time, he will hold his wastes to avoid soiling his bed. It is your responsibility to make sure he isn't left too long.

The crate will also be your Beagle puppy's place of refuge.

Introduce your Beagle puppy to the crate at an early age to help him get used to his new environment. The crate will help him develop bowel and bladder control.

If he's tired, hurt, or sick, allow him to go back to his crate to sleep or hide. If he's overstimulated or excited, put him back in his crate to calm down.

Because the crate physically confines the puppy, it can also prevent some unwanted behaviors such as destructive chewing or raiding the trash cans. When you cannot supervise the puppy or when you leave the house, put him in his crate and he will be prevented from getting into trouble.

Photo by Isabelle Francais

Put your Beagle's crate in a location where he will feel safe and secure, such as in your kitchen. If he feels isolated, he will be more apt to cry or behave in a destructive manner.

Introducing the Crate

Introduce your puppy to the crate by propping open the door and tossing a treat inside. As you do this, tell your puppy, "Go to bed!" Let him go inside to get the treat, investigate the crate, and come and go as he wishes. When he's comfortable with that, offer him his next meal in the crate. Once he's in, close the door behind him. Let him out when he's through eating. Offer several meals in the same fashion in order to show your puppy that the crate is a pretty neat place.

After your Beagle puppy is used to going in and out for treats and meals, start feeding him back in his normal place again and go back to offering a treat for going into the crate. Tell him, "Sweetie, go to bed," and then give him his treat.

Don't let your puppy out of the crate after a temper tantrum. If he starts crying, screaming, throwing himself at the door, or scratching at the door, correct him verbally, "No, quiet!" or simply close the door to the room and walk away. If you let him out during or after a tantrum, you will simply teach him that temper tantrums work. Instead, let him out when you are ready to let him out and when he is quiet.

Crate Location

The ideal place for the crate

Photo by Isabelle Francais

Paper training is an effective method for teaching your puppy how to relieve himself inside of the house. At some point, he should be retrained to relieve himself outside.

beagle

is in your bedroom, within arm's reach of the bed. This will give your Beagle eight uninterrupted hours with you while you do nothing but sleep. In these busy times, that is quality time!

Having you nearby will give your Beagle puppy a feeling of security, whereas exiling him to the laundry room or backyard will isolate him. He will be more apt to cry, whine, chew destructively, or get into other trouble because he is lonely or afraid.

Having the crate close at night will save you some wear and tear, too. If he needs to go outside during the night (and he may need to for a few weeks), you will hear him whine, and you can let him out before he has an accident. If he's restless or bored, you can rap on the top of his crate and tell him to be quiet without getting out of bed.

PAPER TRAINING

One of the most common methods of housetraining a puppy is paper training. The puppy is taught to relieve himself on newspapers and then, at some point, is retrained to go outside. Paper training teaches the puppy to relieve himself in the house. Is that really what you want your Beagle to know?

Teach your Beagle what you want him to know now and later as an adult. Take him outside to the place where you want him to relieve himself and tell him, "Sweetie, go potty." (Use any word you'll be comfortable saying.) When he has done what it is he needs to do, praise him.

Don't just open the door and send your puppy outside. How do you know that he has relieved himself? Go out with him so that you can teach him the command, praise him when he does it, and know he is done and that it's safe to let him back inside.

PUNISHMENT

Do not try and housetrain your puppy by correcting him for relieving himself in the house. If you scold him or rub his nose in his mess, you are not teaching him where he needs to relieve himself—instead you are teaching him that you think going potty is wrong. Because he has to go, he will then become sneaky about it, and you will find puddles and piles in strange places. Keep in mind that the act of relieving himself is very natural; he has to do this. Instead of concentrating on correction, emphasize the praise for going in the right place.

Photo by Isabelle Francais

Establishing a routine for eating, eliminating, playing, walking, training, and sleeping helps your puppy get used to the housetraining process.

If he doesn't relieve himself when you take him outside, this is not a problem. Just put him back in his crate for a little while and take him back outside later. Do not let him run around the house—even supervised—if he has not relieved himself outside.

Successful housetraining is based on setting your Beagle puppy up for success rather than failure. Keep accidents to a minimum and praise him when he does relieve himself where he should go.

ESTABLISH A ROUTINE

Beagles, like many other dogs, are creatures of habit and thrive on a routine.

Housetraining is much easier if there is a set routine for eating, eliminating, playing, walking, training, and sleeping. A workable schedule might look like this:

• **6:00 am**—Dad wakes up and takes the puppy outside. After the puppy relieves himself, Dad praises him and brings him inside. Dad fixes the puppy's breakfast, offers him water, and then sends him out in the backyard while Dad goes to take his shower.

• **7:00 am**—Mom goes outside to play with the puppy for a few minutes before getting ready for work. Just before she leaves, she brings the puppy inside, puts him in his crate, and gives him a treat.

- **11:00 am**—A dog-loving neighbor who is retired comes over. He lets the puppy out of his crate and takes him outside. The neighbor is familiar with the puppy's training, so he praises the puppy when he relieves himself. He throws the ball for the puppy, pets him, and cuddles him. When the puppy is worn out, he puts him back in his crate and gives him a treat.
- **3:00 pm**—Daughter comes home from school and takes the puppy outside. She throws the ball for the puppy, picks up after him, and then takes him for a walk. When they get back, she brings the puppy inside to her bedroom while she does her homework.
- **6:00 pm**—Mom takes the puppy outside to go potty, praises him, and then feeds him dinner.
- **8:00 pm**—After Daughter plays with the puppy, she brushes him and then takes him outside to go potty.
- **11:00 pm**—Dad takes the puppy outside for one last trip before bed.

The schedule you set up will have to work with your normal routine and lifestyle. Just keep in mind that your Beagle puppy should not remain in the crate

THERE ARE NO ACCIDENTS

If the puppy relieves himself in the house, it is not his fault. It's yours. That means the puppy was not supervised well enough or he wasn't taken outside in time. The act of relieving himself is very natural to the puppy, and the idea that there are certain areas where relieving himself is not acceptable is foreign to the puppy. His instincts tell him to keep his bed clean, but that's all. You need to teach him where you want him to go and to prevent him from going in other places. That requires supervision on your part.

for longer than three to four hours at a time, except during the night. In addition, the puppy will need to relieve himself after waking up, after eating, after playtime, and every three to four hours in between.

LIMIT THE PUPPY'S FREEDOM

Many puppies do not want to take the time to go outside to relieve themselves because everything exciting happens in the house. After all, that's where all the family members are. If your Beagle puppy is like this, you will find him sneaking off somewhere—behind the sofa or to another room—to relieve himself. By limiting the

By limiting a puppy's freedom, you can prevent him from getting into trouble. Baby gates and crates can be very effective in keeping your Beagle safe.

Photo by Isabelle Francais

puppy's freedom, you can prevent some of these mistakes. Close bedroom doors and use baby gates across hallways to keep him close. If you can't keep an eye on him, put him in his crate or outside.

HOUSEHOLD RULES

As has been mentioned before, it's important to start teaching your Beagle puppy the household rules you wish him to observe as soon as possible. Your eight- to ten-week-old puppy is not too young to learn, and by starting early, you can prevent him from learning bad habits. When deciding what

PATIENCE, PATIENCE, AND MORE PATIENCE

Beagle puppies need time to develop bowel and bladder control. Establish a routine that seems to work well for you and your puppy and then stick to it. Give your puppy time to learn what you want and time to grow up. If you stick to the schedule, your puppy will progress. However, don't let success go to your head. A few weeks without a mistake doesn't mean your Beagle puppy is housetrained—it means your routine is working! Too much freedom too soon will result in problems.

TIMING AGAIN

Do you walk your dog when he has to go potty? Many dog owners live in condos and apartments, and the dog must go for a walk to relieve himself. These dogs often learn that the walk is over once they go potty, so they hold it as long as possible so that the walk continues. To avoid this trap, encourage your puppy to relieve himself right away, praise him, and then continue the walk or outing for a little while afterward.

rules you want him to learn, look at your Beagle puppy not as the baby he is now, but as the adult he will grow up to be. Jumping up may be cute as a

puppy, but do you want him to jump up on the neighbor's children or your grandmother when he's an adult?

Some rules you may want to institute could include that he must not jump on people, he must behave when guests come to the house, he should stay out of the kitchen, he should leave the trash cans alone, and he should chew only on his toys.

Teaching your Beagle puppy these rules is not difficult. Be very clear with your corrections. When he does something wrong, correct him with your deep, firm tone of voice, "No jump!" When he does something right, use a higher-

Retractable leashes provide dogs with freedom while allowing the owner complete control. Leashes are available in a wide variety of lengths for all breeds of dog. Photo courtesy of Flexi-USA, Inc.

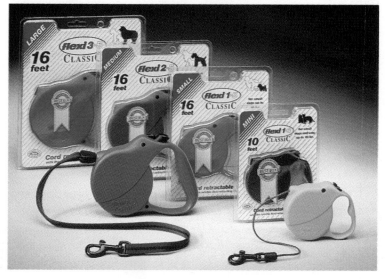

pitched tone of voice, "Good boy to chew on your toy!" You must be very clear—either something is right or it is wrong, there are no shades of gray in between.

ACCEPTING THE LEASH

Learning to accept the leash can be difficult for some puppies. If your Beagle learns to dislike the leash as a young puppy, he may continue to resent it for many years. However, if he learns that the leash is a key to more exciting

Guaranteed by the manufacturer to stop any dog of any size or weight from ever pulling again. It's like having power steering for your dog. Photo courtesy of Four Paws.

things, he will welcome the leash.

Soon after you bring your puppy home, put a soft buckle collar on his neck. Make sure it's loose enough to come over his head in case he gets tangled up in something. Give him a day or two to get used to the collar. Then, when you are going to be close by and can supervise him, snap the leash onto the collar and let him drag it behind him. As he walks around, he will step on the leash, feel it tug on his neck, and in doing so, will get used to the feel of it.

After two or three short sessions like this, you can teach your puppy to follow you on the leash. Have a few pieces of a soft treat that your puppy enjoys (soft so that it is easily chewed). Hold the leash in one hand and the treats in another. Show him the treat and back away a few steps as you tell your puppy, "Let's go! Good boy!" When he follows you a few steps, praise him and give him the treat. Beagle puppies are usually very easily motivated by food, and when he learns a treat is being offered, he should follow you with no problem.

Repeat two or three times and then stop for this training session. Reward your puppy by giving him a tummy rub or by throwing the ball to him a few times.

Photo by Isabelle Francais

The car can be a frightening place for a puppy, because a ride in the car was the first strange thing to happen to him after he was taken from his mother and littermates. Help your puppy understand that the car is fun and enjoyable.

After two or three training sessions like this, make it more challenging by backing up slowly or quickly, or by making turns. If he gets confused or balks, make it simple again until he's willingly following you again.

IF YOUR PUPPY BALKS

If your puppy balks, do not use the leash to drag him to you. This will cause him to dig his feet in and apply the brakes. Instead, kneel down, open your arms wide, and encourage him to you with, "Hey, Sweetie, here! Good boy!" When he dashes to your lap, praise him and tell him what a wonderful puppy he is! Then try the exercise again.

INTRODUCING THE CAR

Many puppies are afraid of the car because a ride in the car was the first strange thing to happen to them when they were taken from their mother and littermates. The car also takes them to the veterinarian's office, another strange place where someone in a white coat pokes them, prods them, and gives them vaccinations. You

Photo by Isabelle Francais

Social handling exercises can help your Beagle become more relaxed and comfortable while you groom him.

don't want this fear of the car to grab hold. You want your puppy to understand that riding in the car is something fun to do.

Start by lifting your puppy into the car and handing him a treat. As soon as he finishes the treat, lift him down and walk away. Repeat this simple exercise several times a day for a few days. Lift him into the car, give him a treat, let him eat it, and then let him explore the car for a few minutes. After he has sniffed around, give him another treat, let him eat it, then lift him down and walk away. Continue this training for a week or two, depending on how nervous your puppy is in the car.

When your puppy is expecting a treat in the car, put his crate in the car and strap it down securely. Put your puppy in his crate, give him a treat, and then start the car's engine. Back down the driveway and then back up to the house. Stop the engine, give your puppy a treat, and let him out of his crate and the car.

The next time, take a drive down the street and back. Then go around the block. Increase the distances and times of the drives very gradually. Keep in mind that you want your puppy to expect good things in the car, not scary things. Your Beagle puppy will have a lifetime of car rides ahead of him and life will be much nicer if he enjoys the rides.

END ON A HIGH NOTE

Always end these (and all) training sessions on a high note. If your Beagle puppy is worried, scared, or confused, help him do something right and then end the training session with that praise. Never end the training session at a negative point in the training or that will affect his outlook toward training later.

SOCIAL HANDLING

Your Beagle puppy cannot care for himself—you must be able to brush and comb him, bathe him, check his feet for cuts and scrapes, and clean his ears. Your Beagle puppy doesn't understand why you need to do these annoying things to him, and he may struggle when you try to care for him. This social handling exercise will help teach your puppy to accept your care.

Sit down on the floor with your puppy and have him lie down between your legs. He can lie on his back or on his side, just let him get comfortable. Start by giving him a slow, easy tummy rub. The idea is to relax him. If your movements are fast and vigorous, you'll make him want to play, so keep it slow and gentle. If he starts to struggle, tell him calmly, "Easy. Be still." Restrain him gently if you need to do so.

When your puppy is relaxed, start giving him a massage. Start at his neck and ears, gently rubbing all around the base of each ear and working down the neck to the shoulders. Continue over his body, gently massaging it while at the same time you check him for cuts, scratches,

Photo by Isabelle Francais

Most dogs are easily excited. If your Beagle has too much energy, help him relax by giving him a gentle massage. This not only calms him down, but also allows you to spend quality time with your pet.

lumps, bumps, bruises, fleas, ticks, or any other problems that need to be taken care of. Once your puppy has learned

It's important that your dog learns how to sit still during grooming. A well-trained dog will be easier to work with.

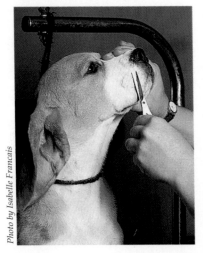

Photo by Isabelle Francais

to enjoy this handling, during the massage you can clean his ears, wash out his eyes, trim his toenails, or do anything else that you need to do.

RELAX!

You can also use the social handling exercise to relax your puppy when he's overstimulated. If you let him in from the backyard and he's full of Beagle energy, don't chase him down or try to correct him. Instead, sit down on the floor and invite him to join you. (Use a treat to get him to come to you if you need some extra incentive.) Once he's come to you, lay him down and begin the massage. He will relax and calm down, and in the process, you are also giving him the attention he needs.

The Basic
OBEDIENCE
Commands

THE TEACHING PROCESS

Although Beagles are an intelligent breed, you cannot simply tell your Beagle to do something and expect him to understand your words. Training is a process that begins with teaching your dog that certain words have meaning and that you would like him to follow your directions. Your Beagle, however, doesn't understand why you want him to do these things—after all, why should he sit? He doesn't know why sitting is so important to you. Therefore, training is a process.

Show Your Dog

First of all, you want to show your dog what it is you want him to do and that there is a word—a human spoken sound—associated with that action or position. For example, when teaching him to sit, you can help him into position as you tell him, "Sweetie, sit." Follow that with praise, "Good boy to sit!" even if you helped him into position.

You will follow a similar pattern when teaching your dog

Showing your dog what to do along with a verbal command helps him to better understand what you are trying to teach him.

most new things. If you want him off the sofa, you can tell him, "Sweetie, off the furniture," as you take him by the collar and pull him off. When he's off the furniture, tell him, "Good boy to get off the furniture."

Praise

Praise him every time he does something right, even if you help him do it. Your Beagle will pay more attention and try harder if he is praised for his efforts. However, don't praise

Photo by Isabelle Francais

Praise is a key factor in the training process. Your dog will pay more attention and try harder if his efforts are recognized.

beagle

him when it's undeserved. Beagles are intelligent dogs and will quickly figure this out. Instead, give enthusiastic praise when he makes an effort and does something right for you.

Correct

Do not correct your dog until he understands what it is you want him to do. After he understands, is willing to obey the command, and then chooses not to do it, you can correct him with a deep tone of voice, "Sweetie, no!" or a quick snap and release of the collar. Use *only* as much correction as is needed to get his attention and *no more*. With corrections, less is usually better as long as your dog is responding.

Timing

The timing of your praise, corrections, and interruptions is very important. Praise him *as* he is doing something right. Correct him *when* he makes the mistake. Interrupt him *as* he starts to stick his nose into the trash can. If your timing is slow, he may not understand what you are trying to teach him.

Be Fair

Beagles resent corrections that are too harsh or unfair. They will show this resentment

USE INTERRUPTIONS

Interrupt incorrect behavior as you see it happen. If your dog is walking by the kitchen trash can and turns to sniff it, interrupt him, "Leave it alone!" If you tell him to sit, and he does sit but then starts to get up, interrupt him, "No! Sit." By interrupting him, you can stop incorrect behavior before or as it happens.

by refusing to work, by planting themselves and refusing to move, or by fighting back.

Interruptions and corrections alone will not teach your Beagle. They are used to stop undesirable behavior or actions at that moment. Your Beagle learns much more when you reward good behavior, so stop the behavior you don't want but lavishly praise the actions you want him to continue.

THE BASIC COMMANDS

Sit and Release

The sit is the foundation command for everything else your Beagle will learn. When your Beagle learns to sit and sit still, he learns to control himself. He learns there are consequences to his actions. This is a very big lesson.

The sit is also a good

The sit command is the foundation for every command that your Beagle will learn. Learning to sit enables him to control himself and behave in an acceptable manner.

alternative action for problem behavior. Your Beagle cannot sit still and jump on you both. He can do one or the other; therefore, learning to sit still for praise can replace jumping up on people for attention. He can't knock his food bowl out of your hand if he's sitting still, waiting patiently for his dinner. You can fasten his leash to his collar more easily if he's sitting still. This is a practical, useful command.

There are two basic methods you may try to teach your Beagle to sit. Some dogs do better with one technique than with the other, so try both and see which is better for your Beagle.

Hold your Beagle's leash in your left hand and have some treats in your right hand. Tell your Beagle, "Sweetie, sit!" as you move your right hand with the treat from his nose over his head toward his tail. He will lift his head to watch your hand. As his head goes up and back, his hips will go down. As he sits, praise him, "Good boy to sit!" and give him a treat. Pet him in the sitting position.

When you are ready for him to get up, tap him on the

This demonstrates the sit and release command. When you are ready for your dog to release the sit, tap him gently on the shoulder as you tell him to release.

SIT, PLEASE!

Once your Beagle understands the sit command and is responding well, start having him sit for things that he wants. Have him sit before you hook his leash to his collar when going for a walk. Have him sit before you give him a treat, give him his meals, or throw his ball.

shoulder as you tell him, "Release!" Each exercise needs a beginning and an end. The sit command is the beginning and the release command tells him he is done and can move now. If he doesn't get up on his own, use your hands on his collar to walk him forward.

If your Beagle is too excited by the treats to think (and some Beagles are like that) put the treats away. Tell your Beagle to sit as you place one hand under his chin on the front of the neck as you slide the other hand down his hips to tuck under his back legs. Gently shape him into a sit as you give him the command, "Sweetie, sit." Praise him and release him.

If your dog wiggles around as you try to teach this exercise, keep your hands on him. If he pops up, interrupt that action.

An obedient dog will be able to sit on command. When your Beagle fully understands the sit command and responds well, have him sit for things that he wants, such as treats.

Photo by Isabelle Francais

The down command also teaches your dog self-control. Although it's not easy for an energetic dog to control his actions, it's a lesson that he must learn.

ONE COMMAND

Don't keep repeating any command. The command is not, "Sit! Sit, sit, *sit,* please sit. SIT!" If you give repeated commands for the sit, your Beagle will assume that carries on to everything else. Tell him one time to sit and then help him do it.

With a deep, firm tone of voice say, "Be still!" When he responds and stops wiggling, praise him quietly and gently.

Down

The down exercise continues one of the lessons the sit command started—self-control. It is hard for many energetic, bouncy young Beagles to control their own actions, but it is a lesson all must learn. Practicing the down exercise teaches your Beagle to lie down and be still.

Start with your Beagle in a sit. Rest one hand gently on his shoulder and have a treat in the other hand. Let him smell the treat and then tell him, "Sweetie, down" and take the treat straight down to the ground in front of his front paws. As he follows the treat down, use your hand on his shoulders to encourage him to lie down. Praise him, give him the treat, and then have him hold the position for a moment. Release him in the same way you did from the

Using a treat is an effective method for teaching your Beagle the basic commands.

sit; pat him on the shoulder, tell him, "Release!" and let him get up.

If your dog looks at the treat as you make the signal but doesn't follow the treat to the ground, simply scoop his front legs up and forward as you lay him down. The rest of the exercise is the same.

As your Beagle learns what the down command means, you can have him hold it for a few minutes longer before you release him, but do not step away from him yet. Stay next to him and if he's wiggly, keep a hand on his shoulder to help him stay in position.

Once each day, have your Beagle lie down, and before you release him, roll him over for a tummy rub. He will enjoy the tummy rub, relax a little, and learn to enjoy the down position. This is especially important for young Beagles that want to do anything *but* lie down and hold still.

Teach your Beagle that the stay command means to hold still. An open-handed gesture with the palm toward your dog's face signals that you want him to stay.

Stay

When your Beagle understands both the sit and down commands, you can introduce him to the stay exercise. You want to convey to your Beagle that the word "stay" means "hold still." When your dog is sitting and you tell him to stay, you want him to remain in the sitting position until you go back to him and release him. When you tell him to stay while he's lying down, you want him to remain lying down until you go back to him to release him from that position. Eventually, he will be able to hold the sit position for several minutes and the down for even longer.

BE CLEAR

Make sure you are very clear to your dog what you want him to do. Remember that something is either right or wrong to your dog—it's not partly right or partly wrong. Be fair with your commands, your praise, and your corrections.

Photo by Isabelle Francais

As your dog learns how to stay, you can gradually increase the time you ask him to hold it. If he makes a lot of mistakes or moves often, it's possible that he doesn't understand the command completely.

beagle

Start by having your Beagle sit. With the leash in your left hand, use the leash to put a slight bit of pressure backward (toward his tail) as you tell him, "Sweetie, stay." At the same time, use your right hand to give your dog a hand signal that will mean stay—an open-handed gesture with the palm toward your dog's face. Take one step away and at the same time, release the pressure on the leash.

If your dog moves or gets up, tell him "No!" so that he knows he made a mistake, and put him back into position. Repeat the exercise. After a few seconds, go back to him and praise him. Don't let him move from the position until you release him. Use the same process to teach the stay in the down position.

With the stay commands, you always want to go back to your Beagle to release him. Don't release him from a distance or call him to come from the stay. If you do either of these, your dog will be much less reliable on the stay. He will continue to get up from the stay because you will have taught him to do exactly that. When teaching the stay command, you want your Beagle to learn that stay means "hold this position until I come

back to you to release you."

As your Beagle learns the stay command, you can *gradually* increase the time you ask him to hold it. However, if your dog is making a lot of mistakes or moving often, you are either asking your dog to hold it too long or your dog doesn't understand the command yet. In either case, go back and reteach the exercise from the beginning.

Increase the distance that you move away from your dog very gradually, too. Again, if your dog is making a lot of mistakes, you're moving away too quickly. Teach everything very gradually.

USING THE STAY COMMAND

You can use the stay command around the house. For example, in the evening while you're watching a favorite television show, have your Beagle lie down at your feet while you sit on the sofa. Give him a toy to chew on and tell him, "Sweetie, stay." Have him do a down/stay when you have visitors so that he isn't jumping all over your guests. Have him lie down and stay while the family is eating so that he isn't begging under the table. There are a lot of practical uses for the stay—just look at your normal routine and see where this command can work for you.

You want your Beagle to be able to ignore distractions and focus his attention on you. The watch me command is a good way to accomplish this.

and release of the leash. When he does control himself, praise him enthusiastically.

Watch Me

The watch me exercise teaches your Beagle to ignore distractions and pay attention to you. This is particularly useful when you're out in public and your dog is distracted by children playing or dogs barking behind a fence.

Start by having your Beagle sit in front of you. Have a treat in your right hand. Let him sniff the treat and then tell him, "Sweetie, watch me!" as you take the treat from his nose up to your chin. When his eyes follow the treat in your hand and he looks at your face, praise him, "Good boy to watch me!" and give him the treat. Then release him from the sit. Repeat it again exactly the same way two or three times and then quit for that training session.

Because this is hard for young, bouncing Beagles, practice it first at home when there are few distractions. Make sure your dog knows it well before you take him outside and try to practice it with distractions. However, once he knows it well inside, then you need to try it outside.

When your Beagle understands the stay command but chooses not to do it, you need to let him know the command is not optional. Many young, wiggly Beagles want to do anything except hold still; however, holding still is very important to Beagle owners. Correct excess movement first with your voice, "No! Be still! Stay!" and if that doesn't stop the excess movement, use a verbal correction and a snap

The heel command helps your Beagle to walk nicely by your side.

Take him out in the front yard (on leash, of course) and tell him to watch you. If he ignores you, take his chin in your left hand (the treat is in your right) and hold his chin so that he looks at your face. Praise him even though you are helping him do it.

When he will watch you out front with some distractions, then move on to the next step. Have him sit in front of you and tell him to watch you. As he watches you, take a few steps backward and ask him to watch you while you are walking together. Praise him when he does. Try it again. When he can follow you six or seven steps and watch you at the same time, make it more challenging—back up and turn to the left or right, or back up faster. Praise him when he continues to watch you.

Heel

You want your Beagle to learn that heel means "walk by my left side, with your neck and shoulders by my left leg, and

When teaching your dog how to heel, don't hesitate to walk forward and then back away. This can sometimes be the best way to get his attention on you.

maintain that position." Ideally, your Beagle should maintain that position as you walk slowly or quickly, turn corners, or weave in and out through a crowd.

To start, practice a "watch me" exercise to get your dog's attention on you. Back away from him and encourage him to watch you. When he does, simply turn your body as you are backing up so that your dog ends up on your left side, and continue walking. If you have done it correctly, it is one smooth movement so you and your dog end up walking forward together with your dog on your left side.

Let's walk through it in slow motion. Sit your dog in front of you and do a "watch me." Back away from your dog and encourage him to follow you. When he's watching you, back up toward your left and as you are backing, continue turning that direction so you and your dog end up walking forward together. Your dog should end up on your left side (and you should end up on your dog's right side).

If your dog starts to pull forward, simply back away from him and encourage him to follow you. If you need to do so, use the leash with a snap-and-release motion to make the dog follow you. Praise him when he does.

Don't hesitate to go back and forth—walking forward and then backing away—if you need to do so. In fact, sometimes this can be the best exercise you can do to get your dog's attention on you.

When your dog is walking nicely with you and paying attention, then you can start eliminating the backing away. Start the heel with your Beagle sitting by your left side. Tell him, "Sweetie, watch me! Heel." Start walking. When he's walking nicely with you, praise him. However, if he gets distracted or starts to pull, simply back away from him again.

The come command is one of the most important commands that your Beagle will learn. It is not only useful around the house, but it could help save your dog's life someday.

Come

The come command is one of the most important commands your Beagle needs to learn. Not only is the come command important around the house in your daily routine, but it could also be a lifesaver some day, especially if he decides to dash toward the street when a car is coming. Because the come command is so important, you will use two different techniques to teach your dog to come to you when you call him.

With a Treat

The first technique will use a sound stimulus and a treat to teach your Beagle to come when you call him. Take a small plastic container (such as a margarine tub) and put a handful of dry dog food in it. Put the lid on and shake it. It should make a nice rattling sound.

Have the shaker in one hand and some good dog treats in the other. Shake the container, and as your Beagle looks at it and you, ask him, "Sweetie, cookie?" Use whatever word he already knows means treat. When you say, "Cookie," pop a treat in his mouth. Do it again. Shake, shake, "Sweetie, cookie?" and pop a treat in his mouth.

The sound of the container, your verbal question, and the

DON'T WORRY

Some people have reservations about this technique because they are worried that the dog will not come to them when they don't have a treat. First of all, you will use two different techniques to teach the come command, and only one technique uses the treats. Second, even with this technique, you will eventually stop using treats. However, by using this technique when first introducing the come command, you can produce such a strong, reliable come response, it's worth all of your efforts.

treat are all becoming associated in his mind. He is learning that the sound of the container equals the treat—an important lesson! Do this several times a day for several days.

Then, with him sitting in front of you, replace the word "cookie" with the word "come." Shake the container, say "Sweetie, come!" and pop a treat in his mouth. You are rewarding him even though he didn't actually come to you—he was still sitting in front of you. However, you are teaching him that the sound of the shaker now equals the word come and he still gets the treat, which is another important lesson. Practice this several times a day for several days.

When your Beagle is happy to hear the shaker and is drooling to get a treat, start calling him from across the room. Shake the container as you say, "Sweetie, come!" When he dashes to you, continue to give him a treat as you praise him, "Good boy to come!" Practice this up and down the hallway, inside and outside, and across the backyard. Make it fun and keep up with the treats and the verbal praise.

The Come with a Long Line

The second method to teach your dog to come to you uses a long leash or a length of clothesline rope. Because Beagles are athletic and fast, have a line at least 30 feet in length. Fasten the line to your Beagle's collar and then let him go play. When he is distracted by something, call him to you, "Sweetie, come!" If he responds and comes right away, praise him.

DON'T USE THE COME COMMAND TO PUNISH

Never call your dog to come to you and then punish him for something he did earlier. Not only is the late punishment always ineffective, but unfair punishment will teach your dog to avoid you when you call him. Keep the come command positive all the time.

USING A SOUND STIMULUS

Do you remember those silent dog whistles that used to be advertised in comic books? There was nothing magical about those whistles except that they were so high-pitched, dogs could hear them but people couldn't. The container we're using to teach the come command works on the same principle that the silent dog whistle used. It's a sound stimulus you can use to get the dog's attention so that you can teach him. By teaching him to pay attention to the sound of the shaker and that the sound of the shaker means he's going to get a treat, we can make the come command that much more exciting. Your dog will be more likely to come to you (especially when there are distractions) if he's excited about it.

If he doesn't respond right away, do *not* call him again. Pick up the line, back away from him, and using the line, make him come to you. Do not give him a verbal correction at this time, because he may associate the verbal correction with coming to you. Instead, simply make him come to you even if you have to drag him in with the line.

Let him go again and repeat the entire exercise. Make sure you always praise him when he does decide to come to you. If he is really distracted, use the shaker and treats along with the long line, especially in the early stages of the training. You can always wean him from the treats later—right now let's make the come command work.

Don't allow your Beagle to have freedom off the leash until he is grown up enough to handle the responsibility and is very well trained. Many dog owners let their dog off leash much too soon, and the dogs learn bad habits that their owners wish they hadn't learned. Each time your dog learns that he can ignore you or run away from you, it reinforces the fact that he can. Instead, let him run around and play while dragging the long line. That way you can always regain control when you need it.

USE IT OR LOSE IT!

The best way to make this training work for you and your Beagle is to use it. Training is not just for those training sessions; instead, training is for your daily life. Incorporate it into your daily routine. Have your Beagle sit before you feed him. Have him lie down and stay while you eat, sit and stay at the gate while you take the trash out, or do a down/stay when guests come over. Use these commands as part of your life. They will work much better that way.

All About
FORMAL
Training

Many dog owners will not admit that their dog needs training. "He does everything I ask," they say. Yet when asked specific questions about behavior, the answer changes. A trained Beagle won't jump up on people, dash out the open door, or raid the garbage can.

Dog owners benefit from training, too. During training, you learn how to teach your Beagle and how to motivate him so that he wants to be good. Then you can encourage good behavior.

WHY IS TRAINING IMPORTANT?

When you decided to add a Beagle to your family, you probably did so because you wanted a companion, a friend, and a confidant. You may have wanted a dog to go for walks with you, to run along the beach, to catch tennis balls, and to hike in the mountains. You may have wanted your children to have the same relationship with a dog that you remember from your childhood. To do any of these things, your Beagle will need training.

Training your dog involves much more than the traditional sit, stay, down, and come commands. This Beagle gets a lesson in group training.

Finding the right training program for your dog can be difficult. Researching different training techniques and methods can help narrow down the choices.

You also learn how to prevent problem behavior from happening and how to correct the inevitable mistakes.

Dog training is much more than the traditional sit, down, stay, and come. Dog training means teaching your Beagle that he's living in your house, not his. It means you can set some rules and expect him to follow them. It will not turn your Beagle into a robot, instead it will teach your Beagle to look at you in a new light. Training will cause you to look at him differently, too. Training is not something you do *to* your Beagle—it's something you do together.

TRAINING METHODS

If you talk to 100 dog trainers (someone who trains dogs) or dog obedience instructors (someone who teaches the dog owner how to teach his dog) and ask them how they train, you will get 100 different answers. Any trainer or instructor who has been in the business for any period of time is going to work out a method or technique that works best for her. Each method will be based on the trainer's personality, teaching techniques, experience, and philosophy regarding dogs and dog training. Any given method may work wonderfully for one trainer but fail terribly for another.

Because there are so many different techniques, styles, and methods, choosing a particular instructor may be difficult. It is important to understand some of the different methods so that you can make a good decision.

Compulsive Training

Compulsive training is regarded as a method of training that forces the dog to behave. This is usually a correction-based training style, sometimes with forceful corrections. This training is usually used with law enforcement and military dogs and can be quite effective with hard-driving, strong-willed dogs. Many pet dog owners do not like this style of training and often feel it is too rough.

Inducive Training

This training is exactly the opposite of compulsive training. Instead of being forced to do something, the dog is induced or motivated toward proper behavior. Depending on the instructor, there are few or no corrections used. This training works very well for most puppies, for softer dogs, and sometimes for owners who dislike corrections of any kind.

Unfortunately, this is not always the right technique for all Beagles. Many Beagles will take advantage of the lack of corrections and discipline.

Some very intelligent dogs with very dominant personalities (including many Beagles) look upon the lack of discipline as weakness on your part and will then set their own rules which, unfortunately, may not be the rules you wish to have.

Somewhere in the Middle

The majority of trainers and instructors use a training method that is somewhere in between both of these techniques. An inducive method is used when possible, while corrections are used when needed. Obviously, the range can be vast, with some trainers leaning toward more corrections and others using as few as possible.

FINDING AN INSTRUCTOR OR TRAINER

When trying to find an instructor or trainer, word-of-mouth referrals are probably the best place to start. Because anyone can place an advertisement in the newspaper or yellow pages, the ad itself is no guarantee of quality or expertise. However, happy customers will demonstrate their experience with well-behaved dogs and will be glad to tell you where they received instruction.

Photo by Isabelle Francais

Be sure that the instructor you choose is qualified and knowledgeable about Beagles and enjoys training them.

However, experience alone is not the only qualification. Some people that have been training for years are still teaching exactly the same way they did many years ago and have never learned anything new.

Ask the instructor about Beagles. What does she think of the breed? Ideally, she should be knowledgeable about the breed, what makes them tick, and how to train them. If she doesn't like the breed, go elsewhere.

Ask the instructor to explain her training methods. Does this sound like something you would be comfortable with? Ask if there are alternative methods used. Not every dog

Have you admired a neighbor's well-behaved dog? Ask where they went for training. Call your veterinarian, local pet store, or groomer and ask who they recommend. Make notes about each referral. What did people like about this trainer? What did they dislike?

Once you have a list of referrals, start calling the instructors and asking each one a few questions. How long has she been teaching classes? You will want someone with experience, of course, so that she can handle the various situations that may arise.

When searching for an instructor or trainer, be sure to inquire about their background, skills, and preferred methods of training.

Photo by Isabelle Francais

Training helps build a trusting and affectionate relationship with your dog. It also helps your dog to become a well-behaved companion and friend.

will respond the same way, and every instructor should have a backup plan.

Does the instructor belong to any professional organizations? The National Association of Dog Obedience Instructors (NADOI) and the Association of Pet Dog Trainers (APDT) are two of the more prominent groups. Both of these organizations publish regular newsletters to share information, techniques, new developments, and more. Instructors belonging to organizations such as these are more likely to be up-to-date on training techniques and styles, as well as information about specific dog breeds.

Make sure that the instructor will be able to help you achieve your goals. For example, if you want to compete in obedience trials, that instructor should have experience in that field and knowledge of the rules and regulations of that competition.

After talking to several trainers or instructors, pick a few and ask if you can watch their training sessions or classes. If they say no, cross them off your list. There should be no reason why you cannot attend one class to see if you will be comfortable with this instructor and her style of

BUILDING A RELATIONSHIP

Training helps build a relationship between you and your dog. This relationship is built on mutual trust, affection, and respect. Training can help your dog become your best friend—a well-behaved companion that is a joy to spend time with and that won't send your blood pressure sky-high!

teaching. As you watch the class, see how the trainer handles her students' dogs. Would you let her handle your dog? How does she relate to the students? Are they relaxed? Do they look like they're having a good time? Are they paying attention to her?

After talking to the instructor or trainer and watching a class, you should be able to make a decision as to which class you want to attend. If you're still undecided, call the instructor back and ask a few more questions. After all, you are hiring her to provide a service and you must be comfortable with your decision.

GROUP CLASSES OR PRIVATE LESSONS?

There are benefits and drawbacks to both group classes and private lessons. In group classes, the dog must learn to behave around other distractions, specifically the other dogs and people in class.

One of the benefits of a group training class is that your dog gets used to behaving properly around other distractions. It also serves as a support group for dog owners.

beagle

65

Before you begin training with your Beagle, decide what goals you want him to accomplish. Then you can find a training program to help you achieve those goals.

Because the world is made up of lots of things capable of distracting your Beagle, this can work very well. In addition, a group class can work like group therapy for dog owners. The owners can share triumphs and mishaps and can encourage and support one another. Many friendships have begun in group training classes.

The drawback to group classes is that for some dogs, the distractions of a group class are too much. Some dogs simply cannot concentrate at all, especially in the beginning of training. For these dogs, a few private lessons may help enough so that the dog can then join a group class later. Dogs with severe behavior problems—especially aggression—should bypass group classes for obvious reasons. Private lessons—one-on-one training with the owner, dog, and instructor—are also good for people with a very busy schedule who may otherwise not be able to do any training at all.

Puppy Class

Puppy or kindergarten classes are for puppies over 10 weeks but not over 16 weeks of age. These classes are usually half obedience training and half socialization, because both of these subjects are very important for puppies. The puppy's owner also learns how

---

GOALS FOR YOUR BEAGLE

What do you want training to accomplish? Do you want your Beagle to be calm and well behaved around family members? Do you want him to behave himself out in public? Would you like to participate in dog activities and sports? There are an unlimited number of things you can do with your Beagle, and it's up to you to decide what you would like to do. Then you can find a training program to help you achieve those goals. As you start training, talk to your trainer about them so she can guide you in the right direction.

Photo by Isabelle Francais

This agile Beagle has fun going through the tire jump. There are classes to prepare you and your dog for various competitions.

to prevent problem behavior from occurring and how to establish household rules.

Basic Obedience Class

This class is for puppies that have graduated from a puppy class, for puppies over four months of age that haven't attended a puppy class, or for adult dogs. In this class, the dog and their owners work on basic obedience commands such as sit, down, stay, come, and heel. Most instructors also spend time discussing problem prevention and problem solving, especially the common problems like jumping on people, barking, digging, and chewing.

Dog Sports Training

Some instructors offer training for one or more of the various dog activities or sports. There are classes to prepare you for competition in obedience trials, conformation dog shows, flyball, agility, or hunting field trials. Other trainers may offer training for non-competitive activities such as therapy dog work.

ADVANCED TRAINING

Advanced training classes vary depending upon the instructor. Some offer classes to teach you to control your dog off leash, some emphasize dog sports, and others may simply continue basic training skills. Ask the instructor what she offers.

Problem
PREVENTION
and Solving

Beagles are not unusually destructive puppies. They can get into trouble and chew up a slipper or two, but do not exhibit anything near what is normal destructive behavior for some other breeds. The problem behavior that gets most Beagles into hot water is barking, baying, or howling. Beagles like to make sure the world is awake when they are!

This is very natural behavior for Beagles; they bay while they're hunting. In fact, they were required to because that's how the Master of the Hounds knew where the pack was. Many of the behaviors that dog owners consider problems—barking, digging, chewing, jumping up on people, and so on—aren't problems to your Beagle. In fact, they are very natural behaviors to your Beagle. Beagles like to jump up

Behaviors that you might consider problems, such as digging or jumping, are natural behaviors to a dog. However, most of these actions can be prevented or at least controlled with the proper training.

Training can play an important part in preventing and controlling problem behavior. It also reinforces to your dog that you are a kind and caring leader.

on people to greet people face to face. Dogs dig because the dirt smells good or because there's a gopher in the yard. Dogs bark to verbalize something just as people talk. All of the things that you

consider problem behaviors are very natural behaviors to your dog. However, most problem behavior can be worked with and either prevented, controlled, or in some cases, stopped entirely.

WHAT YOU CAN DO

Prevent Problems from Happening

Because so many of the things we consider problems are natural behaviors to your Beagle, you need to prevent as many of them from happening as you reasonably can. Put the garbage cans away so that he never discovers that it is full of good-tasting surprises. Make sure the kids put their toys away so that your Beagle can't chew them to pieces. It's much easier to prevent a problem from happening than it is to break a bad habit later.

Problem prevention might require that you fence off the garden, build higher shelves in the garage, or maybe even build your Beagle a dog run.

Part of preventing problems from occurring also requires that you limit your dog's freedom. A young puppy or untrained dog should never have unsupervised free run of the house, because there is

---

TRAINING

Training can play a big part in controlling problem behavior. A fair, upbeat, yet firm training program teaches your dog that you are in charge, and that he is below you in the family pack. Training should also reinforce his concept of you as a kind, calm, caring leader. In addition, your training skills give you the ability to teach your dog what is acceptable and what is not.

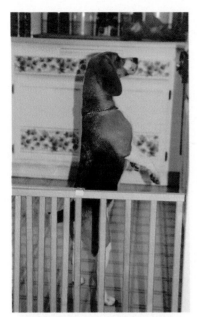

Dogs are very curious animals and if given the chance, they can get into mischief. Putting up a baby gate can help keep your Beagle confined when you cannot supervise him.

problems can cause a behavior change, as can hyperactivity, hormone imbalances, and a variety of other health problems.

If your dog's behavior changes, make an appointment with your veterinarian. Tell your vet why you are bringing the dog in—don't just ask for an exam. Tell your vet that your Beagle has changed his behavior, tell him what the behavior is, and ask if he could do an exam for any physical problems that could lead to that type of behavior.

Don't automatically assume your dog is healthy. If a health problem is causing the behavior change, training or behavior modification won't make it better. Before you begin any training, talk to

simply too much he can get into. Instead, keep him close to you and close off rooms. If you can't watch him, put him into his run or out in the backyard.

Health Problems

Some experts feel that 20 percent of all common behavior problems are caused by health problems. A bladder infection or a gastrointestinal upset commonly causes housetraining accidents. Medications and thyroid

---

A DOG RUN

A dog run is not a dog prison; instead, it is a safe place for him where he can stay while he's unsupervised. He should have protection from the sun and weather, unspillable water, and a few toys in his dog run. Don't put him in his run as punishment and never scold him in his run. Instead, give him a treat or a toy and leave a radio on to quiet, gentle music in a nearby window.

Before you begin any training, make sure that your dog has had a thorough exam and is up-to-date with all of his vaccinations.

Photo by Isabelle Francais

your veterinarian. Once health problems are ruled out, then you can start working with the problem.

Nutrition

Nutrition can play a part in causing or solving behavior problems. If your dog is eating a poor-quality food or if he cannot digest the food he is being fed, his body may be missing some vital nutrients. If your Beagle is chewing on rocks or wood, is chewing the stucco off the side of your house, or is grazing on the plants in your garden, he may have a nutritional deficiency of some kind.

Food for puppies should be nutritionally complete to allow for healthy growth and strong bones. Make sure that the puppy food you choose contains only the highest quality ingredients. Photo courtesy of Nutro Products, Inc.

Proper nutrition is imperative to your dog's health. Veterinarians recommend elevated feeders to help reduce stress on your dog's neck and back muscles. The raised platform also provides better digestion while reducing bloating and gas. Photo courtesy of Pet Zone Products, Ltd.

Some dogs develop a type of hyperactivity when fed a high-calorie, high-fat dog food. Other dogs have food allergies that may show up as behavior problems. If you have any questions about the food your dog is eating, talk to your veterinarian.

Play

Play is different from exercise, although exercise can be play. The key to play is laughter. Researchers know that laughter is wonderful medicine and that it makes you feel better. When you laugh, you feel differently about the world around you.

Laughter and play have a special place in your relationship with your Beagle.

Beagles can be very silly and you should take advantage of that. Laugh at him and with him. Play games that will make you laugh. Play is also a great stress reliever and you should make time for play when you are having a hard time at work. Play with your Beagle after training sessions.

EXERCISE

Exercise is just as important for your Beagle as it is for you. Exercise works the body, uses up excess energy, relieves stress, and clears the mind. How much exercise is needed depends on your dog and your normal routine. A fast-paced walk might be enough for an older Beagle, but a young, healthy Beagle might need a good run or fast-paced game of fetch.

Sometimes dogs get into trouble intentionally because they feel ignored. To these dogs, any attention—even corrections or yelling—is better than no attention at all. If you take time to play with your dog regularly, you can avoid some of these situations.

DEALING WITH SPECIFIC PROBLEMS

Jumping on People

At one time or another, just about every Beagle owner has to deal with their dog jumping up on people. You can, however, control the jumping by emphasizing the sit command. If your Beagle is sitting, he can't jump up. By teaching him to sit for petting, praise, treats, and his meals, you can teach him that the sit is important and that everything he wants will happen only when he sits.

Use the leash as much as you can to teach your Beagle to sit. Small-but-solid muscular dogs, Beagles can be tough to hold onto unless you have something to grab, and the leash is your best training tool. When you come home from work, don't greet your dog until you have a leash and collar in hand. As your dog greets you, slip the collar

Jumping up on people is not a desirable behavior. You can deal with this problem by emphasizing the sit command.

over his head. Then you can help him sit. If he tries to jump, snap and release the leash and add a verbal correction, "No jump! Sit!" Of course, as with all of your training, praise him when he sits.

When you are out in public, make sure your Beagle sits before any of your neighbors or friends pet him. Again, use your leash. If he won't sit still, don't let anyone pet him, even if you have to explain your actions. "I'm sorry but I'm trying to teach him manners and he must sit before he gets any petting," will be a sufficient explanation.

The key to correcting

jumping up is to make sure the bad behavior is not rewarded. If someone pets your Beagle when he jumps up, that action has been rewarded. However, when he learns that he only gets attention when he's sitting, it will make sitting more attractive to him.

Digging

If your backyard looks like a military artillery range, you need to concentrate first on preventing this problem from occurring. If you come home from work to find new holes in the lawn or garden, don't correct your dog then. He probably dug the holes when you first left in the morning and a correction ten hours later won't work.

Instead, build him a dog run and leave him there during the day. If you fence off one side of your yard alongside your house, you might be able to give him a run that is 6 feet wide by 20 feet long. That's a great run. Let him trash this section to his heart's content—that's his yard.

When you are home and can supervise him, you can let him have free run of the rest of your yard. If he starts to get into

Dogs need exercise and play to use up their energy and stimulate their mind. A dog run is a good idea if you can't be home to supervise your dog.

Photo by Isabelle Francais

beagle

trouble, you can use your voice to interrupt him, "Hey! What are you doing? Get out of the garden!"

The destructive dog also needs exercise, training, and playtime every day to use up his energy, stimulate his mind, and give him time with you. Most importantly, don't let this dog watch you garden. If you do, he may come to you later with all of those bulbs you planted earlier!

The Barker

Unfortunately, Beagles are often problem barkers, although the noise they make often isn't really barking but howling instead. A Beagle left alone for many hours each day may find that barking and howling gets him attention, especially if your neighbors yell at him. To your Beagle, negative attention is better than no attention at all.

Start teaching him to be quiet when you're at home with him. When your Beagle starts barking, tell him, "Quiet!" When he stops, praise him. When he understands what you want, go for a short walk outside, leaving him home. Listen, and when you hear him start barking, come back and correct him. After a

few corrections, when he seems to understand, ask your neighbor to help you. Go into your front yard and ask your neighbor to come out to talk. Have the kids out front playing. When your dog barks because he's feeling left out, go back and correct him. Repeat as often as you need to until he understands.

You can reduce your dog's emotional need to bark if you make coming home and leaving home as quiet and low-key as possible. When you leave the house, don't give him hugs or tell him repeatedly to be a good dog. That will simply make your exit more emotional. Instead, give him attention an hour or two prior to the time you leave, and when it's time for you to go, just go. When you come home, ignore your dog for a few minutes. Then whisper hello to him. Your Beagle's hearing is very good, but to hear your whispers, he is going to have to be quiet and still.

You can also distract your dog when you leave. Take a brown paper lunch bag and put a couple of treats in it— maybe a dog biscuit, a piece of carrot, and a slice of apple. Roll the top over to close it

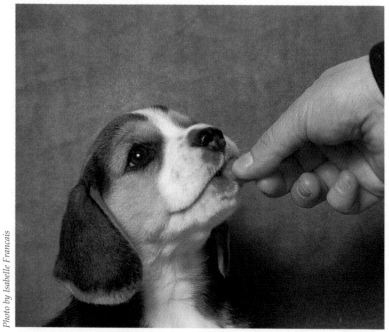

Photo by Isabelle Francais

A good way to distract your dog when you leave the house is to give him some treats to keep him occupied.

and rip a very tiny hole in the side to give your dog encouragement to get the treats. As you walk out the

ONE BEAGLE OR TWO?

If you are gone for many hours each day, you may want to get a second Beagle to keep your first company. Granted, two dogs are twice as much work as one, but Beagles are pack dogs, and one dog left alone for many hours each day is going to be very unhappy. Two dogs can keep each other occupied and reduce your feelings of guilt.

EXTRA HELP

Problem barkers may need extra help, especially if your neighbors are complaining. There are anti-bark collars on the market, several of which are very humane and effective. All are triggered by the dog's barking and administer a correction to the dog. Some collars make a high-pitched sound, one squirts a whiff of citronella, and others administer a shock. I do not recommend the shock collars for most Beagles, because many dogs will panic at this correction. However, the first two collars are quite effective.

door or gate, hand this to your dog. He will be so busy figuring out where the treats are and how to get them, he'll forget you are leaving.

Dashing Through Doors and Gates

This is actually one of the easier behavior problems to solve. Teach your Beagle to sit at all doors and gates, then hold that sit until you give him permission to go through or to get up after you have gone through. By teaching him to sit and to wait for permission, you will eliminate the problem.

Start with your dog on leash. Walk him up to a door. Have him sit, tell him to stay, and then open the door in front of him. If he dashes through, use the leash to correct him (snap and release) as you give him a verbal correction, "No! Stay!" Take him back to his original position and do it again. When he will hold it at this door, go to another door or gate and

If you have a job that requires you to be away from home for long periods of time, you might want to consider getting a playmate for your Beagle. In this case, two Beagles are better than one.

Photo by Isabelle Francais

Your dog should be trained not to dash through doors and gates before you do. The sit command is useful in this situation.

repeat the training procedure.

When he will wait while on leash at all doors and gates, take his leash off and hook up his long line. Fasten one end of the long line to a piece of heavy furniture. Walk him up to the door and tell him to sit and stay. Drop the long line to the ground. With your hands empty, open the door and stand aside. Because your hands are empty (meaning you aren't holding the leash), your Beagle may decide to dash. If he does, the long line will stop him or you can step on the line. Give him a verbal correction, "No! I said stay!" and bring him back to where he started. Repeat the

training session here and at all other doors and gates.

Other Problems

Many behavior problems can be solved or at least controlled using similar techniques. Try to figure out why your Beagle is doing what he's doing (from his point of view, not yours). What can you do to prevent the problem from happening? What can you do to teach your dog not to do it? Remember, as with all of your training, a correction alone will not change the behavior. You must also teach your dog what he can do.

If you still have some problems or if your dog is showing aggressive tendencies, contact your local dog trainer or behaviorist for some help.

RUNNING FREE

If your Beagle does make it out through a door or gate, don't chase him. The more you chase, the better the game, as far as he's concerned. Instead, go get your shaker you used for training the come command. Shake it, "Sweetie, do you want a cookie? Come!" When he comes back to you, you must praise him for coming even though you may want to wring his neck for dashing through the door. Don't correct him, because a correction will make him avoid you even more the next time it happens.

Advanced
TRAINING
and Dog Sports

If you and your Beagle enjoy the time spent together while training, it doesn't have to be over just because you have completed basic obedience training. There is always more to learn. Teach your dog to listen to you off leash. Teach him hand signals, and even some tricks. There is a lot you can do together, including a number of different dog activities and sports. However, before you begin any of these exercises or activities, make sure your Beagle is proficient in all of the basic commands. If he's having trouble with some of

the basic commands, go back and review and practice them.

HAND SIGNALS

When you start teaching hand signals, use a treat in your hand to get your Beagle's attention. Use the verbal command he already knows to help him understand what you are trying to tell him. As he responds, decrease the verbal command to a whisper and emphasize the hand signal.

The difficult part of teaching hand signals is that in the beginning, your dog may not understand that these movements of your hand and arm have any significance. After all, people "talk" with their hands all the time, and our hands are always moving and waving. Dogs learn early to ignore hand and arm movements. Therefore, to make hand signals work, your Beagle needs to watch you. A good treat in the hand making the movement can help.

Down

When you taught your Beagle to lie down by taking the treat from his nose to the

---

USING HAND SIGNALS

Dog owners often think of hand signals as something that only really advanced dogs can respond to, and that is partly right. It does take some training. However, hand signals are useful for all dog owners. For example, if your dog responds to hand signals, you can give him the signal to go lie down while you're talking on the telephone, and you won't have to interrupt your conversation to do so.

ground in front of his front paws, you were teaching him a hand signal. Granted, he was watching the treat in your hand, but he was also getting used to seeing your hand move. Therefore, switching him over from a verbal command to a hand-signal-only command should be easy.

Have your dog sit in front of you. Verbally, tell him, "Down" as you give him the hand signal for down with a treat in your hand, just as you did when you were originally teaching it. When he lies down, praise him and then release him. Practice it a few times.

Now, give him the signal to go down with a treat in your hand, but do not give a verbal command. If he lies down, praise him, give him the treat and release him. If he does not go down, give the leash a slight snap and release down toward the ground, not hard, but just enough to let him know, "Hey! Pay attention!" When he goes down, praise and release him.

When he can reliably follow the signal with no verbal command, make it more challenging. Signal him to lie down when you are across the room, while you're talking to someone, and when there are some distractions around him.

Remember to praise him enthusiastically when he goes down on the signal.

Sit

If you were able to teach your Beagle to sit using the treat above his nose, you were teaching him to sit using a hand signal. If you had to teach him by shaping him into a sit, don't worry, you can still teach him the hand signal.

With your Beagle on leash, hold the leash in your left hand. Have a treat in your right hand. Stand in front of your Beagle and take the treat from his nose upward. At the same time, whisper, "Sit." When he sits, praise him and release him. Try it again. When he is watching your hand and sitting reliably, stop whispering the command and let him follow the signal. If he doesn't sit, jiggle the leash and collar to remind him that something is expected. Again, when he sits, praise him.

Stay

When you taught the stay command you used a hand signal, the open-palmed gesture toward your Beagle's face. This signal is so obvious that your dog will probably do it without any additional training. Have your dog sit or lie down and tell

An obedient and well-behaved dog is a pleasure to have as a companion.

The hand signal for the come command should be broad, easily seen, and clear to your Beagle.

him, "stay" using only the hand signal. Did he hold it? If he did, go back and praise him. If he didn't, use the leash to correct him (snap and release) and try it again.

Come

You want the signal for the come to be a very broad, easily seen signal, one that your dog can recognize even if he's distracted by something. Therefore, this signal will be a wide swing of the right arm, starting with your arm held straight out to your side from the shoulder, horizontal to the ground. The motion will be to bring the hand to your chest following a wide wave, as if you were reaching out to get

your dog and bring him to you.

Start teaching the signal by having the come shaker in your right hand as you start the signal. Shake it slightly— just to get your dog's attention—and then complete the signal. Praise your dog when he responds and comes to you.

If he doesn't respond right away, start the signal again and this time tell him verbally to come as you are making the signal and shaking the shaker. Again, praise him when he comes. Gradually eliminate the verbal command, and when your Beagle is responding well, gradually stop using the shaker.

If your Beagle has trouble responding to the hand signal at first, use a verbal command in conjunction to help him understand.

OFF-LEASH CONTROL

One of the biggest mistakes many dog owners make is to take the dog off the leash too soon. When you take your dog off the leash, you have very little control—only your previous training can control your dog. If you take your dog off leash before you have established enough control or before your dog is mentally mature enough to accept that control, you are setting yourself up for disaster.

Beagles are smart, curious dogs and they love to check out new things, especially new smells. A rabbit was made to chase as far as Beagles are concerned, as well as a butterfly or a bird. More than one Beagle has been so involved in his exploring that he's forgotten to pay attention to his owner's commands.

Before your Beagle is to be allowed off leash (outside of a fenced yard or your backyard), you need to make sure your Beagle's training is sound, which means he should be responding reliably and well to all of the basic commands.

Your Beagle must also be mentally mature, and in some Beagles that might not be until two or even two-and-a-half years of age. He should be past the challenging teenage stage of development. Never take a

Use the long line to teach your Beagle the come command. It also will prepare him for off-leash control.

young adolescent off leash outside of a fenced-in area—that is setting the young dog up for a problem.

Come on a Long Line

The long line or leash was introduced earlier in the section on teaching the come command. It is also a good training technique for preparing your dog for off-leash control. Review that section and practice the come command on the long line until you are positive that your dog understands the come command from 20 to 30 feet away (the length of the long line) and will do it reliably.

Now take him out to play in

This picture demonstrates using the long line to teach the come command. If your dog will not come when you call, you can pull him to you.

a different place that is safe—a schoolyard is good. Let your Beagle drag his long line behind him as you let him sniff and explore. When he's distracted and not paying attention to you, call him to come. If he responds right away, praise him enthusiastically. Tell him what a smart, wonderful dog he is!

If he doesn't respond right away, step on the end of the long line, pick it up, and back away from your dog, calling him again as you use the long line to make him come to you. Don't beg him to come to you or repeat the come command over and over. Simply use the line to make him do it. The come is not an optional command.

Heel

Most places require that dogs in public be leashed; however, teaching your Beagle to heel without a leash is a good exercise. Not only is it a part of obedience competition (for people interested in that sport), but it's a good practical command, too. What would happen if your dog's leash or collar broke when you were out for a walk? Accidents happen, and if your dog has already been trained to heel off leash, disaster can be averted.

To train for the off-leash heel, hook two leashes up to your dog's collar. Use your regular leash as well as a lightweight leash. Do a watch me with treats and then tell your dog to heel. Practice a variety of things: walk slowly and quickly, turn corners, and perform figure eights. When your dog is paying attention well, reach down and unhook his regular leash, tossing it to the ground in front of him. If he bounces up, assuming he's free, correct him with the second leash, "Hey! I didn't release you!" and make him sit in the heel position. Hook his regular leash back up and repeat the exercise.

When he doesn't take advantage of the regular leash being taken off, then tell him to heel and start practicing the heel. Do not use the second leash for minor correction but save it for control. If he tries to dash away, pull from you, or otherwise break the heel exercise, use that second leash and then hook his regular leash back on again.

Repeat this, going back and forth between one leash and two, until he's not even thinking about whether his regular leash is on or not. You want him to work reliably without questioning the leash's control. For some Beagles, this may take several weeks' worth of work.

When he is working reliably,

put the second leash away. Take his regular leash, hook it up to his collar and fold it up. Tuck it under his collar, between his shoulder blades so that it is lying on his back. Practice his heel work. If he makes a mistake, grab the leash and collar as a handle and correct him. When the correction is over, take your hand off.

Expect and demand the same level of obedience off leash that you do on leash. Don't make excuses for off-leash work.

DOG SPORTS

Do you like training your Beagle? If you and your Beagle are having a good time, you may want to try one or more dog activities or sports. There are a lot of different things you

FIELD TRIALS

Beagles are hunting dogs and to a Beagle, there is nothing better than chasing a rabbit. If you would like to work with your Beagle in his instinctive occupation, write to the American Kennel Club (AKC) and ask for information about Beagle field trials. You can also contact a dog trainer in your area and ask if someone is training field hounds locally. Beagle breeders might also know of a field trainer.

Photo by Isabelle Francais

The athletic and energetic Beagle has the ability to excel in many different activities.

can do with your dog. Some are competitive, some are fun, some help others, but what you decide to do depends on you and your dog.

Conformation Competition

The American Kennel Club (AKC) and the United Kennel Club (UKC) both award conformation championships to purebred dogs. The requirements vary between the registries, but basically a championship is awarded when a purebred dog competes against other dogs of his breed

and wins. When competing, the judge compares each dog against a written standard for his breed and chooses the dog that most closely represents that standard of excellence.

This is a very simplistic explanation; however, if you feel your Beagle is very handsome, you might want to go watch at a few local dog shows. Watch the Beagles competing and talk to some of the Beagle owners and handlers. Does your Beagle still look like a good candidate? You will also want to do some reading about your breed and about

Obedience competition is just one of the many activities you and your dog can train to participate in. There are classes available that concentrate on specific dog sports.

conformation competition, and perhaps even attend a conformation class.

Obedience Competition

Obedience competition is a team sport involving you and your Beagle. There are set exercises that must be performed in a certain way, and both you and your dog are judged as to your abilities to perform these exercises.

Both the AKC and the UKC sponsor obedience competitions for all breeds of dog, as do some other organizations, including the Beagle Club of America. There are also independent obedience competitions and tournaments held all over the country.

Before you begin training to compete, write to the sponsoring organization and get a copy of the rules and regulations pertaining to competitions. Go to a few local dog shows and watch the obedience competitions—see

Photo by Karen Taylor

Many Beagles excel in agility, which is a fast-paced sport in which the dog must complete a series of obstacles in a certain amount of time. "Squiggles," owned by Marietta Huber, shows his athletic ability in the high jump.

who wins and who doesn't. What did they each do differently? There are also a number of books on the market specifically addressing obedience competition. You may want to find a trainer in your area who specializes in competition training.

Canine Good Citizen

The Canine Good Citizen (CGC) program was instituted by the AKC in an effort to promote and reward responsible dog ownership. During a CGC test, the dog and owner must complete a series of ten

AGILITY

Agility is a fast-paced sport in which the dog must complete a series of obstacles correctly in a certain period of time, and the dog with the fastest time wins. Obstacles might include tunnels, hurdles, an elevated dog walk, and more. The AKC, the UKC, and the United States Dog Agility Association all sponsor agility competitions. Many Beagles participate in agility for fun and training, and can sometimes even be competitive against faster breeds like Border Collies and Shetland Sheepdogs.

exercises, including sitting for petting and grooming, walking nicely on the leash, and the basic commands sit, down, stay, and come. Upon the successful completion of all ten exercises, the dog is awarded the title CGC.

For more information about CGC tests, contact a dog trainer or dog training club in your area.

Temperament Test

The American Temperament Test Society was founded to provide breeders and trainers with a means of uniformly evaluating a dog's temperament. By using standardized tests, each dog is tested in the same manner. The tests can be used to evaluate potential breeding stock or future working dogs, or can be used simply as a way for dog owners to see how their dog might react in any given situation.

For information about temperament tests in your area, contact a local trainer or dog training club.

Tracking

Beagles have excellent scenting abilities and make natural tracking dogs. The AKC sponsors tracking competitions. For more information, write to

FLYBALL

Flyball is a great sport for dogs that are crazy about tennis balls. Teams of four dogs and their owners compete against each other. Each dog runs down the course, jumps four hurdles, and then triggers the mechanism that spits out a tennis ball. The dog then catches the ball, turns back, jumps the four hurdles again, and returns to his owner. The team to complete the relay first wins. Athletic Beagles can run and jump with the best of dogs, and flyball is a fun sport.

the AKC and ask for their rules and regulations concerning tracking trials.

Therapy Dogs

Dog owners have known for years that our dogs are good for us, but now researchers are agreeing that dogs are good medicine. Therapy dogs are those dogs that go to nursing homes, hospitals, and children's centers to provide warmth, affection, and love to the people who need it most. Beagles are sometimes a little standoffish with strangers, but the Beagles that like people make great therapy dogs. For more information, contact your local dog trainer for information about a group in your area.

Have Some FUN With Your Training

Obedience training has a tendency to be serious. After all, much of this training is teaching your Beagle what his place in the family is and how to control himself. That can be serious stuff.

However, training can also be fun, especially from a Beagle's viewpoint. Games and trick training can challenge your training skills and your Beagle's ability to learn. Once you have taught your dog, you can have a

Beagles are excellent tracking dogs. Make tracking into a fun game so that your dog can utilize his natural abilities.

great time showing off his tricks, amusing your friends, and just plain having fun.

THE COME GAME

This is a great game to show your Beagle puppy how much fun it is to come when called. Two family members sit on the ground or floor across the yard or down the hall-way from each other. Each should have some treats for the puppy. One family member calls the puppy across the yard or down the hall and when the puppy reaches her, she praises the puppy and gives him a treat. She then turns the puppy around so that he's facing the other family member, who calls the puppy. This very simple game can make teaching the come command exciting for the puppy. In addition, kids can play this game too, giving them a chance to participate in the puppy's training.

TRACKING FOR FUN

Most dog owners assume that tracking is something that search and rescue or law enforcement dogs do to find or save people. And it's true, these dogs need tracking skills. But tracking can also be fun for you and your Beagle, and can be something that you practice as a game.

Retrieving games are fun and a great way for your Beagle to get exercise.

First thing in the morning, go out to your yard, an empty schoolyard, or a vacant lot. Have a leash on your Beagle and fasten it to a chest harness (not a neck collar that could hamper his movements). Rub a piece of hot dog on the sole of one shoe and then rub that shoe in the grass, imparting the smell to the grass. Walk forward 20 or 30 feet, scuffing that foot a little, and then place a bit of hot dog on the ground. Jump off your track (a big jump to the side if you're able) and walk back to your dog.

Point to the ground where you started as you tell your dog, "Find it!" When he starts sniffing, let him work it out. If he follows the track, hold the leash but let him move ahead of you—don't interfere. When he finds the treat, praise him.

As he gets better, you can make the track more difficult by adding turns or zigzags. Use the hot dogs for quite a while, though, to make the tracking more fun for him.

RETRIEVING

Most Beagles like to retrieve, but they just don't always understand the need to bring back what they go out after. However, once you teach your Beagle to bring back the toy, retrieving games can be great fun, as well as good exercise.

If your Beagle likes to retrieve, then all you need to do is get him to bring you back the toy. When you throw the toy and he goes after it, wait until he picks it up. Once he has it in his mouth, call him back to you in a happy tone of voice. If he drops the toy, send him back to it. If he brings the toy all the way back to you, praise him enthusiastically.

Don't let him play tug-of-war with the toy. If he grabs it and doesn't want to let go, reach over the top of his muzzle and tell him, "Give," as you press his top lips against his teeth. You don't have to use much pressure, just enough so that he opens his mouth. When he gives you the toy, praise him.

If your Beagle likes to take the toy and run, let him drag his long line behind him while he plays. Then, when he dashes off, you can step on the line and stop him. Once you've stopped him, call him back to you.

THE NAME GAME

The name game is a great way to make your dog think. And don't doubt it for a minute—your Beagle can think! When you teach your Beagle the names of a variety of things around the house, you can then put him to work, too. Tell him to pick up your keys or your purse, or send him after the remote control to the television. The possibilities are unlimited!

Start with two items that are very different, perhaps a tennis ball and a magazine. Sit on the floor with your Beagle and place the two items in front of you. Ask him, "Where's the ball?" and bounce the ball so that he tries to grab it or at least pays attention to it. When he touches it, praise him and give him a treat.

When he is responding to the ball, lay it on the floor and send him after it. Praise and reward him. Now set several different items out with the magazine and ball and send him after the ball again. When he is doing well, start all over again with one of his toys. When he will get his toy, then put the toy and ball out there together and send him after one or the other. Don't correct him if he makes a mistake, just take the toy away from him and try it again. Remember, he's learning a foreign language (yours) at the same time he's trying to figure out what the game is, so be patient.

FIND IT

When the dog can identify a few items by name, you can then start hiding those items so that he can search for them. For example, once he knows the word "keys," you can drop your keys on the floor under an end table next to the sofa. Tell your Beagle, "Find my keys!" and help him look. Ask, "Where are they?" and move him toward the end table. When he finds them, praise him enthusiastically. Beagles use their nose instinctively and are very good at it, so this game should be easy.

As he gets better, make the game more challenging. Make him search in more than one room. Have the item hiding in plain sight or underneath something else. In the beginning, help him, especially when he appears confused. But don't let him give up—make sure he succeeds.

HIDE AND SEEK

This is also an easy one for Beagles because it lets the Beagle

Dogs have a very curious nature. Hiding certain items and letting your Beagle find them is a good way for him to use his scenting abilities.

Photo by Isabelle Francais

Hide-and-seek is another fun game that you can play with your Beagle. This cute pup looks ready to go find his treasure.

Photo by Isabelle Francais

Photo by Isabelle Francais

No matter what tricks you decide to teach your Beagle, he will enjoy spending the time with his favorite friend—you.

use his scenting abilities. Start by having a family member pet your Beagle, offer him a treat, and then walk away to another room. Tell your Beagle, "Find Dad!" and let him go. If he runs right to Dad, praise him. Have different family members play the game and teach the dog a name for each of them so that he can search for each family member.

As he gets better at the game and learns the family member's names, the person hiding will no longer have to pet the dog at the beginning of the game. He can simply go hide. Help your dog initially so that he can succeed, but also encourage him to use his nose and his scenting abilities.

HAVE FUN WITH TRICKS

I taught one of my dogs to play dead and we both had a lot of fun with it. Michi got so good he could pick the phrase "dead dog" out of casual conversation. One day the son of a neighbor of mine had just graduated from the police academy and was very proud of his new uniform. Michi and I were out front, so we went over to congratulate the new police officer. As I shook the police officer's hand, I turned to Michi and asked him, "Would you rather be a cop or a dead dog?" Michi dropped to the ground, went flat on his side, and closed his eyes. The only thing giving him away (showing that he really was having fun) was his wagging tail. Meanwhile, my neighbor's son was stuttering and turning red. He didn't know whether to be offended or to laugh! It was great fun.

SHAKE HANDS

Shaking hands is a very easy trick to teach. Have your dog sit in front of you. Reach behind one front paw and as you say, "Shake!" tickle his leg in the hollow just behind his paw. When he lifts his paw, shake it gently and praise him. When he starts lifting his paw on his own, stop tickling.

WAVE

When your dog is shaking hands reliably, tell him, "Shake. Wave!" and instead of shaking his paw, reach toward it without taking it. Let him touch his paw to your hand but pull your hand away so that he's waving. Praise him. Eventually you want him to lift his paw higher than for the shake and to move it up and down so he looks like he's waving. You can do that with the movements of your hand as he reaches for it. Praise him enthusiastically when he does it right. When he understands the wave, you can stop your hand movements.

ROLL OVER

With your Beagle lying down, take a treat and make a circle with your hand around his nose

---

MAKE UP YOUR OWN TRICKS

What would you and your Beagle have fun doing? Teach him to stand up on his back legs and dance. Teach him to jump through a hula hoop or your arms forming a circle. Teach him to play dead or to sneeze. Trick training is limited only by your imagination and your ability to teach your dog.

---

as you tell him, "Roll over." Use the treat (in the circular motion) to lead his head in the direction you want him to roll. Your other hand may have to help him. Beagles have a big rib cage and it may take some effort on your dog's part to start the roll-over movement.

The things that you can teach your Beagle are limited only by your imagination.

SUGGESTED READING

BOOKS BY T.F.H. PUBLICATIONS

RE317
The Guide to Owning a Beagle
Andrew Vallila
64 pages, 50 full-color photos

JG109
A New Owner's Guide to Training
the Perfect Puppy
Andrew DePrisco
160 pages, 150 full-color photos

JG136
A New Owner's Guide to Beagles
David and Hazel Arnold
160 pages, 150 full-color photos

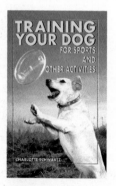

TS258
Training Your Dog for Sports and
Other Activities
Charlotte Schwartz
160 pages, 170 full-color photos